DATE DUE

JUN 2 8 2005		
APR 1 6 2007		
PR102		

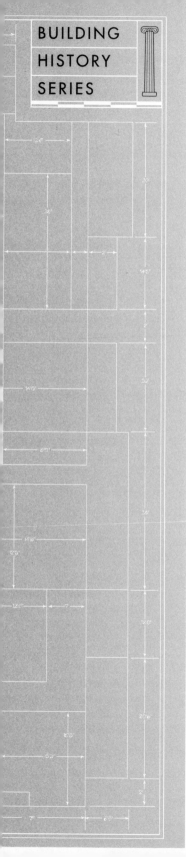

THE

SISTINE CHAPEL

TITLES IN THE BUILDING HISTORY SERIES INCLUDE:

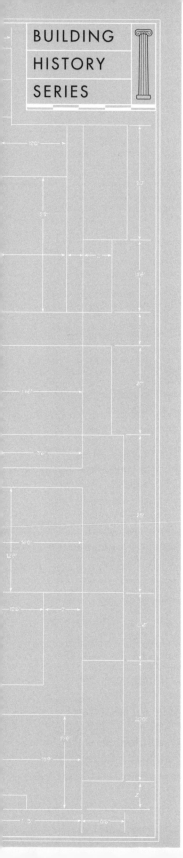

BUILDING
HISTORY
SERIES

THE

SISTINE CHAPEL

by Renee C. Rebman

Lucent Books, Inc., San Diego, California

For Grandma Lucy Zajack Hunter

Library of Congress Cataloging-in-Publication Data

Rebman, Renee C., 1961–
   The Sistine Chapel / Renee C. Rebman.
     p.   cm. — (Building history series)
   Includes bibliographical references and index.
   Summary: Discusses the history of the Sistine Chapel,
including the frescoes, Michelangelo's influence, the Last
Judgment, and modern day restoration.
   ISBN 1-56006-640-7 (lib. bdg. : alk. paper)
   1. Michelangelo Buonarroti, 1475–1564—Juvenile literature.
2. Mural painting and decoration, Renaissance—Conservation and
restoration—Juvenile literature. 3. Mural painting and decoration,
Italian—Conservation and restoration—Vatican City—Juvenile
literature. 4. Cappella Sistina (Vatican Palace, Vatican City)—
Juvenile literature. 5. Vatican City—Buildings, structures, etc.—
Juvenile literature. [1. Sistine Chapel (Vatican Palace, Vatican City)
2. Michelangelo Buonarroti, 1475–1564.] I. Title. II. Series.

ND623.B9 R38 2000
759.5—dc21
                                             99-046399

Contents

FOREWORD

Throughout history, as civilizations have evolved and prospered, each has produced unique buildings and architectural styles. Combining the need for both utility and artistic expression, a society's buildings, particularly its large-scale public structures, often reflect the individual character traits that distinguish it from other societies. In a very real sense, then, buildings express a society's values and unique characteristics in tangible form. As scholar Anita Abromovitz comments in her book *People and Spaces*, "Our ways of living and thinking—our habits, needs, fear of enemies, aspirations, materialistic concerns, and religious beliefs—have influenced the kinds of spaces that we build and that later surround and include us."

That specific types and styles of structures constitute an outward expression of the spirit of an individual people or era can be seen in the diverse ways that various societies have built palaces, fortresses, tombs, churches, government buildings, sports arenas, public works, and other such monuments. The ancient Greeks, for instance, were a supremely rational people who originated Western philosophy and science, including the atomic theory and the realization that the earth is a sphere. Their public buildings, epitomized by Athens's magnificent Parthenon temple, were equally rational, emphasizing order, harmony, reason, and above all, restraint.

By contrast, the Romans, who conquered and absorbed the Greek lands, were a highly practical people preoccupied with acquiring and wielding power over others. The Romans greatly admired and readily copied elements of Greek architecture, but modified and adapted them to their own needs. "Roman genius was called into action by the enormous practical needs of a world empire," wrote historian Edith Hamilton. "Rome met them magnificently. Building tremendous, indomitable amphitheaters where eighty thousand could watch a spectacle, baths where three thousand could bathe at the same time."

In medieval Europe, God heavily influenced and motivated the people, and religion permeated all aspects of society, molding people's worldviews and guiding their everyday actions. That spiritual mindset is reflected in the most important medieval structure—the Gothic cathedral—which, in a sense, was a model of heavenly cities. As scholar Anne Fremantle so elegantly phrases it, the cathedrals were "harmonious elevations of stone and glass reaching up to heaven to seek and receive the light [of God]."

Our more secular modern age, in contrast, is driven by the realities of a global economy, advanced technology, and mass communications. Responding to the needs of international trade and the growth of cities housing millions of people, today's builders construct engineering marvels, among them towering skyscrapers of steel and glass, mammoth marine canals, and huge and elaborate rapid transit systems, all of which would have left their ancestors, even the Romans, awestruck.

In examining some of humanity's greatest edifices, Lucent Books' Building History Series recognizes this close relationship between a society's historical character and its buildings. Each volume in the series begins with a historical sketch of the people who erected the edifice, exploring their major achievements as well as the beliefs, customs, and societal needs that dictated the variety, functions, and styles of their buildings. A detailed explanation of how the selected structure was conceived, designed, and built, to the extent that this information is known, makes up the majority of the volume.

Each volume in the Lucent Building History Series also includes several special features that are useful tools for additional research. A chronology of important dates gives students an overview, at a glance, of the evolution and use of the structure described. Sidebars create a broader context by adding further details on some of the architects, engineers, and construction tools, materials, and methods that made each structure a reality, as well as the social, political, and/or religious leaders and movements that inspired its creation. Useful maps help the reader locate the nations, cities, streets, and individual structures mentioned in the text; and numerous diagrams and pictures illustrate tools and devices that bring to life various stages of construction. Finally, each volume contains two bibliographies, one for student research, the other listing works the author consulted in compiling the book.

Taken as a whole, these volumes, covering diverse ancient and modern structures, constitute not only a valuable research tool but also a tribute to the human spirit, a fascinating exploration of the dreams, skills, ingenuity, and dogged determination of the great peoples who shaped history.

IMPORTANT DATES IN THE BUILDING OF THE SISTINE CHAPEL

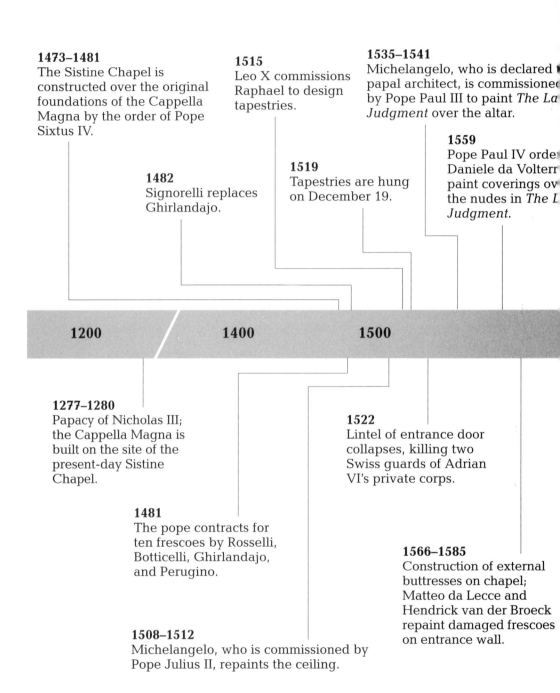

1473–1481
The Sistine Chapel is constructed over the original foundations of the Cappella Magna by the order of Pope Sixtus IV.

1515
Leo X commissions Raphael to design tapestries.

1535–1541
Michelangelo, who is declared papal architect, is commissioned by Pope Paul III to paint *The Last Judgment* over the altar.

1482
Signorelli replaces Ghirlandajo.

1519
Tapestries are hung on December 19.

1559
Pope Paul IV orders Daniele da Volterra paint coverings over the nudes in *The Last Judgment*.

1200   1400   1500

1277–1280
Papacy of Nicholas III; the Cappella Magna is built on the site of the present-day Sistine Chapel.

1522
Lintel of entrance door collapses, killing two Swiss guards of Adrian VI's private corps.

1481
The pope contracts for ten frescoes by Rosselli, Botticelli, Ghirlandajo, and Perugino.

1566–1585
Construction of external buttresses on chapel; Matteo da Lecce and Hendrick van der Broeck repaint damaged frescoes on entrance wall.

1508–1512
Michelangelo, who is commissioned by Pope Julius II, repaints the ceiling.

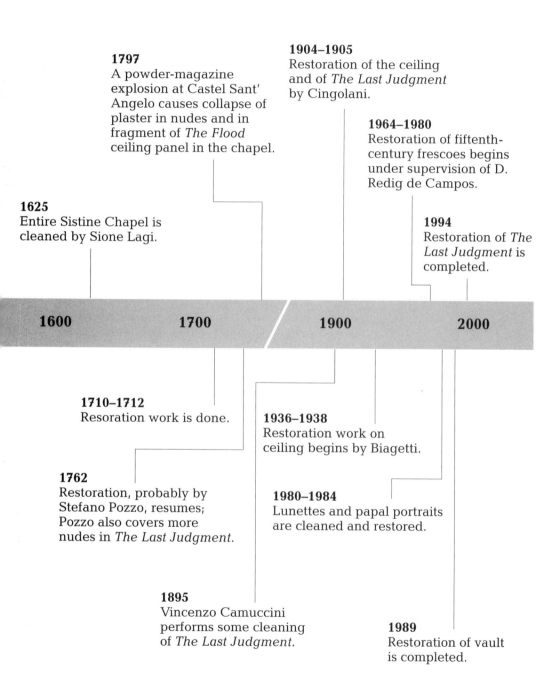

1797
A powder-magazine explosion at Castel Sant' Angelo causes collapse of plaster in nudes and in fragment of *The Flood* ceiling panel in the chapel.

1904–1905
Restoration of the ceiling and of *The Last Judgment* by Cingolani.

1964–1980
Restoration of fiftenth-century frescoes begins under supervision of D. Redig de Campos.

1625
Entire Sistine Chapel is cleaned by Sione Lagi.

1994
Restoration of *The Last Judgment* is completed.

1600 **1700** **1900** **2000**

1710–1712
Resoration work is done.

1936–1938
Restoration work on ceiling begins by Biagetti.

1762
Restoration, probably by Stefano Pozzo, resumes; Pozzo also covers more nudes in *The Last Judgment*.

1980–1984
Lunettes and papal portraits are cleaned and restored.

1895
Vincenzo Camuccini performs some cleaning of *The Last Judgment.*

1989
Restoration of vault is completed.

INTRODUCTION

For over five hundred years, Rome's Sistine Chapel has played a vital role in the rituals of the Catholic Church. Its historical significance, however, rests on its unique place as a repository of masterpieces of art that epitomize and symbolize the artistic achievement of the Italian Renaissance. Its fifteenth- and sixteenth-century carvings, paintings, and frescoes, inseparable from the structure, awe and inspire viewers to the present day. From its inception, only the most celebrated artists of the age—the architect Bramante, the painter and sculptor Michelangelo,

Michelangelo's massive fresco The Last Judgment *dominates the interior of the Sistine Chapel.*

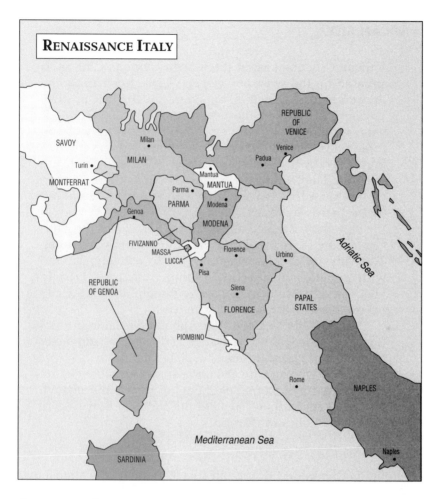

the painter Raphael—were involved in its creation. The story of this revered building—a story of tradition, religion, ego, and the holy men and artistic geniuses who made their dreams a reality —has fascinated the world for centuries.

In 1473, the year construction began, Europe was just emerging from the feudalism of the Middle Ages; a ruling class of nobles still ruled a mostly illiterate class of peasants and the economy was still largely agricultural. The Italian boot was a nonunified collection of city-states that regularly went to war against each other, and few people had the education or funds to devote themselves to artistic projects or patronage. Columbus had not yet sailed to the New World, but trade routes to Asia had been opened and a growing merchant class was beginning to prosper.

VATICAN CITY

Vatican City, the seat of the Roman Catholic Church, is situated on the west bank of the Tiber River in Rome. Recognized as its own independent sovereignty in 1929, Vatican City is the smallest country on earth. It is very private, surrounded by medieval and Renaissance walls on three sides. The southeast side is not walled, but it is distinguished by the famous Square of St. Peter's. There are only three public entrances into Vatican City, and all are closely guarded. An army of more than one hundred Swiss guards serves as security.

St. Peter's Basilica, the Sistine Chapel, and the Vatican museums are visited by millions of tourists each year. The Vatican Library, which is open to scholars, is filled with priceless manuscripts dating from pre-Christian eras.The artwork, architecture, and sculptures of the city eclipse those of any other city on earth.

Vatican City has its own telephone system, radio station, post office, banking system and coinage, and many stores. Nearly all of its goods must be imported.

Within Vatican City, the pope enjoys absolute control (based on the centuries-old belief of papal supremacy). His influence extends beyond the Vatican, however, to Roman Catholics worldwide.

Religion dominated European society, which was almost entirely Christian. One institution, the Roman Catholic Church, headed by the pope as God's representative on earth, influenced the individual's political, religious, and social life from cradle to grave. The church amassed vast wealth in landholdings, taxes, and tithes, and it had the means to commission church construction and works of art, mostly religious art, among the growing community of artists at work in Florence, Rome, and Venice. As patron and all-powerful overseer, the church dictated the content and scope of the literary, artistic, and scientific invention that was taking hold across the continent.

Thus, the center of European culture during the flowering of arts and science known as the Renaissance was the Roman Catholic Church. The center of the church was Rome. The epicenter of church power and authority was the 0.17-square-mile city within a city of monuments, courts, and administrative offices known as the Vatican. And the nucleus of the Vatican was the grand square shared by the pope's apartments, St. Peter's Basilica, and the Sistine Chapel. From that perspective, no other building occupied a more privileged place. Its history begins with an ambitious pope intent on immortalizing himself. As the world now knows, Sixtus IV succeeded beyond his dreams.

THE POPE'S CHAPEL

From the beginning of its construction, the Sistine Chapel was considered an architectural gem among all the buildings in Vatican City, Rome. It was built by the ambitious Pope Sixtus IV in 1473 to provide highly visible proof of the church's unending glory and importance. It also served as a constant reminder of the power and authority of the pope himself.

For the first six years of his papacy, Pope Sixtus used the Cappella Magna, a medieval structure erected by Pope Nicholas III between 1277 and 1280. The Cappella Magna functioned as a keep, the fortified section of a medieval structure, as well as the pope's chapel. Its central location, set in a square around the court of the *pappagallo*, the very center of the ancient apostolic palaces, emphasized its importance. Though it had long served the many needs of the pope and the church, the aging, cramped structure had finally become a hindrance to the smooth conduct of church business and to the special papal masses that took place there throughout the year. It also lacked the splendor befitting a pope.

THE CROWDED PAPAL COURT

The decision-making body of the church, the papal court, met at least forty-two times a year to debate and decide church policy. Their meetings took place in privacy, behind a closed screen that separated them from the rest of the chapel. The Capella Magna simply was no longer big enough to comfortably house the two hundred or more men who made up the papal court. Its members included the pope, the College of Cardinals, senior churchmen, visiting archbishops and bishops, secretaries, notaries and auditors, and other members of the papal household.

This description, written in 1460, gives a clear picture of the overcrowded conditions: "On the floor of the chapel the papal household and others wander around and make so much noise during the Divine Office and sermons that one can scarcely hear what is being said."[1]

It was here, as well, that the College of Cardinals met (upon the death of a pope) to elect a new pope. This most holy ritual, entrenched in tradition and closely guarded secrecy, took place within the crowded confines of the pope's chapel.

The College of Cardinals consisted of up to 120 men, each of whom took an oath upon entering the meeting that he would abide by the rules and maintain absolute secrecy about voting and deliberations. The penalty for disclosing anything about the procedures was automatic excommunication from the church. Members were not permitted any contact with the outside world: They were unable to send or receive messages, letters, or signals from outsiders. During the selection process, the public was locked out and the cardinals locked inside.

The cardinals were seated around the wall of the chapel and given a ballot paper on which was written "Eligo in suumum pontificem"—"I elect as supreme Pontiff . . . ". After writing a name on the paper, the cardinals folded it and one by one approached the altar. At the altar was a communion cup, or chalice, with a paten (a plate made of precious metal) on it. Each cardinal held up his ballot to show that he had voted, then placed it on the paten and slid it into the chalice. When all ballots had been gathered into the chalice, they were counted. The names were read aloud, written on a tally sheet, then joined by a needle onto a length of thread. The ballots and all notes made during the voting were then burned.

A CHAPEL BUILT FOR SECRECY

Secrecy was of key importance during the election of a new pope. The vaults, or reinforced ceilings, constructed below and above the main interior of the Sistine Chapel were difficult to break through and also made the chapel soundproof. These security measures were helpful in discouraging spies who might attempt to sneak into the chapel to hear the proceedings when a new pope was being elected. Conclave rules also dictated the placement of the windows on the chapel: They were required to be built ten yards above the floor to maintain absolute privacy.

The election of a new pope required a two-thirds majority. If, after thirty votes, the two-thirds majority could not be reached, the pope could be chosen by a straight majority. The cardinals voted twice in the morning and once in the afternoon until a decision was made.

The faithful masses waiting on the street cast their eyes to the sky, searching for a plume of smoke to announce the outcome of the voting. Black smoke meant that no decision had been reached. White smoke signaled the election of a new pope.

SPECIAL MASSES

Aside from church business and the election of popes, the Cappella Magna also served as the location for special papal masses—at least twenty-seven per year. By the time of Sixtus, however, the aging chapel could no longer accommodate the growing numbers of church faithful and the popularity of these ceremonial masses. Sixtus was forced to conduct mass in chapels throughout Vatican City. For daily masses he used the Chapel of Nicholas; High Masses were held in Old St. Peter's; and Christmas and Palm Sunday masses were conducted in the Papal Palace of the Vatican.

Tired of conducting mass in overcrowded chapels, Pope Sixtus commissioned a magnificent new chapel.

This traveling from chapel to chapel seemed hardly befitting a man of Sixtus's station. Both proud and stubborn, he ruled his domain with an iron fist. He was a successful military leader capable of ruthlessness in war. His desires became reality. He wanted Rome to become the center of culture and commissioned many paintings and sculptures. He also founded the Vatican Library and was responsible for many building projects in Vatican City.

The construction of a new chapel, which he would call the Sistine Chapel, would end the necessity of the proud pope

POPE SIXTUS

Pope Sixtus was born into a very poor family. While still a child, it was determined that he should become a priest. He was totally devoted to the study of theology and had an intense interest in politics.

Upon becoming pope, he entered into a two-year war with the city of Florence in hopes of overthrowing the city and bringing it under the rule of his nephew, Cardinal Rafael Riario. Florence had many allies, however, and the pope was forced to make peace. This failure, along with hints of a conspiracy by Cardinal Riario that may have led to the assassination of Giuliano de' Medici, a member of the powerful Medici family, were blots on the pope's career.

He then turned all of his attention to improving Rome and Vatican City. He built the Sistine Chapel, founded the Vatican Library, and transformed the unsanitary conditions of Rome, making it clean for the general population. His earlier mistakes, which chiefly involved poor judgment and nepotism, were forgiven. The Sistine Chapel was considered the pinnacle of his success and guaranteed the pope his place in history.

moving from place to place to conduct masses. His congregation would now come to him. And the chapel he proposed would be grand enough to honor his memory for centuries to come.

Driving the Darkness Away

Pope Sixtus planned for his new chapel to be grand in design, decoration, and proportion. In 1473 architect Giovannino de' Olci was commissioned to draw the plans for the new Sistine Chapel. Baccio Pontelli, in charge of Vatican building at the time, was hired to work under de' Olci.

The architect envisioned the chapel as a huge fortress three stories high, towering over the low clustered buildings that made up part of the Vatican complex. Its size would communicate to all the political as well as religious authority the church and its pope sought to command. Unlike the modern papacy, the popes of the time often acted more like secular rulers than spiritual leaders, frequently leading Vatican armies in warfare against neighboring rulers.

Most of the architectural features used were common on other large structures of the time. Among the most important were corbels, or decorative brackets used to support weight; cornices, which were horizontal projections that crowned the outside walls; and crenellations, which were defensive parapets at the top of the walls. The corbels had holes in them to provide openings for throwing burning oil and other projectiles at would-be attackers. This possible defense function was taken seriously because a papal palace in Avignon had been besieged twice during the first years of the century.

De' Olci planned an interior that would be spacious and extravagantly decorated with gilding, marble floors, paintings, and statues. All artwork would illustrate biblical teachings. The

An illustration of the original ceiling of the Sistine Chapel, painted a deep blue and covered with gold stars.

THE ORIGINAL BASEMENT
OF THE CAPPELLA MAGNA IS SAVED

Many studies have tried to determine exactly how much of the original foundations of the Capella Magna were preserved when the Sistine Chapel was built on its site. For example, it is clear on the south wall, below the window level, that the brickwork and a set of stairs descending to the Paradiso are original to the medieval structure. The brick placement, thickness of mortar, and plaster on the walls does not match that of later construction.

Located on the outside facade of the same area are many decorative stone coats of arms. These clearly honor Pope Sixtus as they represent the della Rovere family from which he was descended. They are placed directly into the brick, and the seams of mortar are quite smooth. This indicates that the decorative work was set during new construction rather than added to preexisting walls. The difference between the original and later construction is quite clear.

ceiling, designed by decorative specialist Pier d'Amelia, would be deep blue and covered with a field of gold stars. An elaborate drawing of this design still exists today. The drawing was carefully painted with lapis lazuli, an expensive blue pigment, and was executed with such care that it appears to have been a final copy made specifically for Pope Sixtus's approval. Designs such as this were commonly used on ceilings at the time, and blue and gold were the colors of the influential della Rovere family, from whom Sixtus descended.

The new chapel was built on the site of the Cappella Magna. The above-ground rooms of the Cappella Magna were demolished, but the subterranean rooms were preserved and improved for use in the new chapel. The ten-foot-thick basement walls were reinforced and the rooms improved to serve as storage, housing for holy relics, tombs for saints, and to make room for the Presepio, the nativity where Christ was born.

One of the large cellar rooms, known as the Paradiso, dated back to medieval times. It was preserved and improved by the addition of groin vaults for support and windows to bring light into the space. Aurelio Lippo Brandolini wrote about the improvements after the chapel was completed:

It had been night here, even in the middle of the day; it was a gloomy spot, neither a dwelling nor a fit place for men; it seemed a dark dungeon and unworthy to be a dungeon, appropriate only as a cave intended for use by sheep, not men. Hell was its nickname since one seemed to be living close to the underworld there; in fact, it was hardly a dwelling place at all. But Sixtus drove the darkness away and brought back the light of the sky, and to this place, that had been unaccustomed to it, he gave back the light of day.[2]

THE TOMBS AND THE PRESEPIO

The two lower levels, divided into nine rooms each, were mainly used for storage. The lower levels also served as the burial site of St. Jerome and Pope Pius V, mentor to Pope Sixtus. In addition to housing the tombs, the lower levels were designated as the new location for the Presepio, the ancient chapel that houses the holy relic of the nativity where Christ was born.

Today the Presepio is positioned directly below the altar of the Sistine Chapel, sunken into the lower level and surrounded by a subterranean passageway. Moving the Presepio to the new Sistine Chapel strengthened the chapel's direct link to the Christmas liturgy. Here, the faithful could re-create the Nativity each year. The pope also declared the altar of the chapel to be papal, meaning only the pope was entitled to celebrate mass there. He would share his chapel with no common priests.

Architect Domenico Fontana was commissioned to accomplish the difficult task of moving the Presepio, which was made of poor material and consisted of many pieces. He described the assignment given to him:

> Our Father wanted then, to have transported into . . . [his] chapel that so very sacred and ancient chapel of the Presepio, for which he ordered that I should raise it in its entirety, from the very place where one found it before, in order to maintain the devotion and the memory, entrusting me to use profound diligence and care in execution, and to bring it safely to the place assigned by His Holiness which is in the center of the new chapel seventy palmi away from where it was before.[3]

A painting from the Presepio, the ancient subterranean chapel housing the relic of the Nativity.

A marble tableau of Mary, Jesus, Joseph, and the three Magi was also moved nearby along with a sculptured group of the entire Nativity and other decorative carvings.

Construction of the chapel was probably completed by 1480. The brick chapel is rectangular in shape and measures 133 feet long by 44 feet wide. It is 133 feet high and is roofed by a flattened barrel vault. It is two stories high, with a large attic space above the vault (the main ceiling of the sanctuary) that accesses the corbels. Although its powerful size was impressive compared to other structures in Vatican City, its interior would garner the most interest and praise.

THE CHAPEL INTERIOR

The chapel's inner walls are lined with sixteen large windows that are separated by niches that hold religious figures. Two large east-facing windows above the altar helped fill the chapel with natural light.

The colored-marble inlaid floor is one of the finest examples of the mosaic work known as *opus Alexandrinum*. The marble is arranged in various geometric patterns that help define the processional path (used by the pope) and other areas used for specific purposes. For example, a pattern of six interlocking circles marked the route the pope and his entourage took when entering the chapel's eastern half. A large square defined an area known as the Quadratura, which was surrounded by wooden benches arranged on three sides for the cardinals' use. The rest of the papal court sat in designated spaces according to rank on benches or marble steps and on the floor around the Quadratura. A design of smaller rectangles marked the route to the pope's throne, which was on a raised podium to the left of the altar.

Statues of St. Peter and St. Paul, carved by the artist Leonardo Sormani, stand on either side of the throne wall—the wall directly behind the altar and against which the pope's throne is placed. Likenesses of these two saints appear many times

Large interlocking circles dominate the chapel's mosaic floor design.

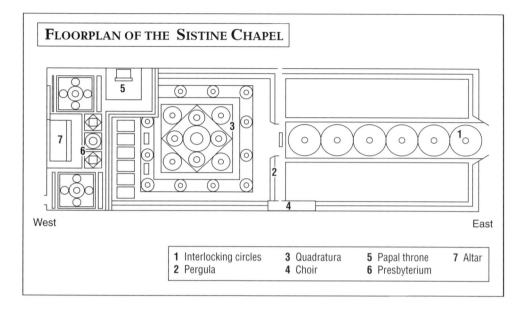

FLOORPLAN OF THE SISTINE CHAPEL

West   East

| **1** Interlocking circles | **3** Quadratura | **5** Papal throne | **7** Altar |
| **2** Pergula | **4** Choir | **6** Presbyterium | |

in the artwork of the chapel, reflecting their significance as founders of the Catholic Church.

THE *PERGULA* AND CHOIR BALUSTRADE

A marble screen, or *pergula*, separated the altar and papal throne from the rest of the congregation and divided the chapel exactly in half. (The *pergula* was moved in the mid-1500s, however, to accommodate the growing papal court.) A beautifully carved marble balustrade, or railing, surrounded the singers' gallery of the choir. The balustrade and *pergula* were carved by Mino da Fiesole, Giovanni Dalmata, and Andrea Bregno, skilled artisans known for their fine marble work. Each of their intricately decorated columns and coordinating chandeliers, which hung above the area, are totally unique in design; not one is repeated.

The walls of the chapel were deliberately left bare with few columns or other architectural elements, so they could be lavishly decorated with fresco. Elaborate frescoes were common in churches and chapels at the time, but those of the Sistine would surpass all and become known throughout history as some of the finest ever executed.

THE WALL FRESCOES

The unforgettable glory the pope sought for his chapel was achieved through the frescoes, which decorated every square inch of the walls of the sanctuary. Fresco was a popular form of wall painting during the fifteenth century and the most difficult to execute. With fresco, the artist merges colored pigments with wall plaster; the process is long and arduous.

The design of the frescoes would encompass three specific areas, which would be decorated in three very different ways. The side walls were to be decorated with a series of gilded frescoes depicting biblical narratives from the lives of Christ and Moses, six from the book of Luke and six from the book of Matthew. Below the narratives there would be faux draperies—that is, frescoes painted to appear to be genuine gold and silver tapestry covered with acorns and oak leaves, the symbols of the pope's family. Above the biblical narratives, portraits of the first thirty-two popes would be executed in chronological order of their papacy, encompassing several centuries.

THE ARTISTS

Preparation for the Sistine fresco work probably began in 1481. The pope commissioned some of Italy's most famous painters for the work of decorating the chapel. All were based in Florence and many were well known for their work in oils as well as fresco. Among the artists chosen for the job was Pietro Perugino, possibly the most successful painter in Italy at the time. Perugino had worked for Pope Sixtus on another Vatican project. Others included Sandro Botticelli, known for his ability to give life to characters from ancient mythology; Domenico Ghirlandajo, master of the fresco style of painting; and Bernardino di Betto di Biago (known as Pinturicchio), a renowned colorist. Luca Signorelli, known for his interest in the anatomy and action of the human figure, was also contracted for the work. Piero di Cosimo, Fra Diamante, and Bartolomeo della Gatta all assisted in minor capacities on the frescoes.

There are no records indicating why Pope Sixtus chose the particular artists he did, but historians surmise that his decision was, to some extent, politically motivated. The pope, heading the Vatican army, had been at war with the city of Florence from 1477 to April 1478. Choosing a group of Florentine painters to work on his chapel could have been a gesture meant to cement peace with his former enemies. By extending this honor to the city's most famous sons, the pope in essence extended an olive branch.

PERUGINO AND BOTTICELLI

The two most famous artists who worked on the wall frescoes of the Sistine Chapel were Perugino and Botticelli.

Perugino, baptized Pietro di Cristoforo Vannucci, studied in Florence. He was very famous and worked throughout Italy. One of his best works is considered to be an altarpiece he painted for the Church of Sant' Agostino in Perugia, the city from which he derived his name. He was a prolific painter, but unfortunately few of his works survive to this day. His style of painting, known as early classicism, is considered to have set the stage for Renaissance art. Early classicism is characterized by sumptuous detail and a polished, precise presentation.

Sandro Botticelli was considered a leading Florentine painter, and he had his own workshop by age twenty-five. Other than the period in which he went to Rome to work for the pope, he spent his entire life in Florence. Botticelli worked extensively for the powerful Medici family (who also sponsored Michelangelo), painting many of their portraits. He is best known for his clear, rhythmic lines, delicate colors, lavish decoration, and poetic feeling. One of his most famous paintings is the mythological telling of the *Birth of Venus*.

A self-portrait by Sandro Botticelli, a Florentine painter who worked on the chapel.

OPPORTUNITY AND PRESTIGE

The Sistine Chapel was the most desired and prestigious art project in all of Rome. The chance to work on such a grand scale with master artists on so important a building was an opportunity not to be missed. Unnamed artists came from far and wide in hopes of gaining a position as assistant to the masters. As many as a dozen men may have actually earned that privilege.

Prestige was the primary motivation but not the only one. Some accounts suggest the artists were to be paid according to their skill level, the talent shown in the execution of the frescoes, and according to the pope's satisfaction with the finished product. Exactly what the pope's criteria were remains unknown. Historian Giorgio Vasari recounted that the pope "did not understand much about these things, although he took great delight in them."[4]

Both Perugino and Botticelli were at the height of their fame when they were brought to the chapel. Opinions vary as to which of these two artists was in charge of the project. According to Vasari, Botticelli "had acquired in Florence, and outside it, such a measure of fame, that Pope Sixtus having built a chapel in his palace in Rome, and wishing to have it painted, ordered that he should be made the head man or overseer."[5] But most historians credit Perugino as being in charge of the project because his fame at the time far exceeded even Botticelli's renown.

Regardless of who was in charge, the work progressed quickly. Pope Six-

Pietro Perugino, a renowned Italian painter of the time, was most likely in charge of the wall frescoes.

tus, who was already in his late sixties, wanted to see the chapel interior completed in his lifetime. To accomplish this, the artists worked long hours, side by side, evenly spaced on a series of scaffolding. They were assigned two or more sections to enable them to work freely on a large area. Even with so many artists, the work proved exhausting.

THE PROCESS OF FRESCO

Fresco is the most enduring form of painting because pigment is applied directly to wet plaster and actually becomes part of it as it dries. It is also one of the most involved forms of painting, requiring a great deal of preparation. For the Sistine Chapel, the artists first sketched full-scale drawings of their design, known as cartoons. Some cartoons were quite detailed because fresco painting left little room for error. Corrections were not easily made, so the cartoon was extremely important.

The wall or area to be frescoed was scraped clean and was coated with a preparatory layer of plaster called the *arriccio*. The *arriccio* provided a solid base for the fresco. Sometimes as many as four or five layers of *arriccio* would be applied in an attempt to even out the surface to be painted.

Then the final layer of plaster, or *intonaco,* was carefully applied. The *intonaco* consisted of finely ground and cleaned limestone mixed with pozzolana (ground volcanic powder) and water. To achieve the desired consistency and texture, sand, marble dust, and even animal hair would sometimes be added.

The *intonaco* was applied in an area large enough to accommodate the day's work, which was known as the *giornate*. Since pigments were applied to the plaster while it was wet, an artist only had eight to twelve hours to paint the *giornate*. The size of the *giornate* varied greatly depending on an artist's skill and the complexity of the design of the fresco.

POUNCING AND INDIRECT INCISION

The cartoons were then transferred to the *giornate* by one of two methods: pouncing or indirect incision. Pouncing was more commonly used because it caused less visible damage to the *intonaco*. During the pouncing method, the cartoon was placed over a thin sheet of paper fastened directly onto the wet plaster. A stylus, or sharp, pen-shaped instrument, then punctured a series of small holes along the outline of the design of the cartoon.

The cartoon was then hit with a small bag of charcoal dust which penetrated the holes and left the outline in the plaster. The cartoons and guide sheets were usually destroyed by the process. Pouncing leaves the surface of the *intonaco* flat and undamaged.

The indirect incision method was quicker to execute than pouncing. In this method the cartoon was laid directly onto the wet plaster and traced with a metal or ivory stylus to produce the outline. Tracing too deeply could ruin the surface of the plaster and any tracing would be visible in the finished product.

The artist was then ready to apply the pigments. Fresco work is difficult not only because of the preparatory work but also because the artist does not have the ability to move the paint freely as is possible when working in oils. In fresco, paint is generally applied in layers to achieve shadows and depth. Corrections are not easily made. There are two ways to make corrections to a fresco; *pentimento* and *a secco*.

In *pentimento* the section of the fresco to be corrected is scraped off and the plaster removed. New *arriccio* is plastered in and the artist essentially starts from scratch in filling in the correction.

In an *a secco* correction the artist merely paints over part of the fresco after it has dried. While this will look effective at first, the *a secco* portion will not be permanent or waterproof because it does not bind with the original surface and eventually can flake off.

THEMES AND PLACEMENT

Just as there existed a precise method to the style of painting, there also existed a method to the placement of the painted scenes on the chapel walls. Following a common medieval practice, Old Testament narratives were positioned on the north wall. Each is captioned, telling which story it depicts. As the Sistine Chapel is oriented with the altar wall to the west rather than to the east, these scenes were painted on what was known as the liturgical north, the left side of the altar as one faces it. The New Testament scenes were on the opposite, or right, wall. The paintings were meant to be viewed in a clockwise manner. Two scenes, *St. Paul with His Epistle and a Young Man Writing* and *St. Peter Entering Rome*, were painted on the altar wall.

Each fresco consisted of two or more scenes within a painted frame. Each scene told its own story. These traditional biblical scenes also included warlike images, which were said to mirror the military and political exploits of Pope Sixtus. For example,

CONTVRBATIO·MOISI·LEGIS·SCRIPTAE·LATOR

The wall fresco The Punishment of Corah, *by Botticelli, is thought to represent the sanctity of the priesthood and the power of the pope.*

The Punishment of Corah was said to represent the pope's many war victories and his divine papal power. The panel depicts Corah's demise after he challenged the authority of Moses and Aaron to command under God. Above the panel is the Latin inscription, "No one can assume the honor [of the priesthood] unless he is called by God, just as Aaron was."[6] This inscription is meant to emphasize the sanctity of the priesthood. *The Cleansing of the Leper* panel was said to commemorate the pope's rebuilding of the old Hospital S. Spirito.

Other famous biblical stories found among the Sistine Chapel frescoes include *The Temptation*, the story of Adam and Eve in the Garden of Eden; *The Passage of the Red Sea*, depicting Moses parting the waters; and *The Last Supper*, depicting Christ's final meal with his disciples before his crucifixion.

THE STYLE OF THE PANELS

Historians cannot say for certain which artists painted which frescoes (since they did not sign their work.) The uniformity of figure sizes, placement of the horizon, amount of background and landscape, and color palette—no doubt done intentionally to create a unified presentation—makes identification of the work of individual artists difficult. Historians have, nevertheless, compared the frescoes with other work done by artists of the time who are known to have worked on the chapel. This has allowed experts to make educated guesses about who painted many of the frescoes. In some cases, a single fresco reveals the work of more than one artist.

Other panels reveal techniques identified with a particular artist. For example, Perugino has been credited with the two scenes on the altar wall: *St. Paul with His Epistle and a Young Man Writing* and *St. Peter Entering Rome*. Botticelli is credited with painting *The Temptation*. Signorelli, who began work as an assistant to Perugino, is believed to have assisted on *The Giving of the Keys to St. Peter*. Historians believe that Signorelli later executed two panels on his own: *The Testament of Moses* and *Fight over the Body of Moses*. *The Passage of the Red Sea* is attributed to Piero di Cosimo, and *The Last Supper* is attributed to Rosselli.

Historians believe that painter Luca Signorelli assisted on The Giving of the Keys to St. Peter.

A side fresco by Botticelli depicts a scene from the life of Moses, a subject not commonly seen in religious art of the time.

HISTORICAL INFORMATION PRESERVED

The chapel frescoes have provided art historians with valuable information about art techniques, painting styles, and even lifestyles of the period. Artists often included in their paintings the faces and figures of their contemporaries, whom they dressed in contemporary fashions. Friends of the artists, cardinals, and even bishops can be seen in the frescoes. *The Cleansing of the Leper*, for example, contains portraits of the pope's nephews, including a young Giuliano della Rovere, who later became pope and assumed the name Julius II. This practice has provided a record of people, architecture, costumes, and even armor of the late 1400s. The frescoes also serve as historical references by depicting famous buildings in their backgrounds.

UNIQUE IN DECORATION

Although much of the artwork was done in a style common for the times, two aspects of the side frescoes are unique to the Sistine Chapel. From medieval times through the Renaissance, it was very unusual to find any paintings in chapels depicting the life of Moses. Most were decorated with Creation scenes from Genesis, the first book of the Bible.

Another unique feature of the side frescoes of the Sistine Chapel is the quantity of gilding, or thin gold overlay, that was

THE RAPHAEL TAPESTRIES

Frescoes are not the only great artwork in the Sistine Chapel. In 1515 Pope Leo X commissioned the painter Raphael to design a series of tapestries to be hung over the faux painted draperies during grand liturgical ceremonies.

In two years' time, Raphael designed and painted ten large cartoons, which were sent to Brussels for weaving. These huge tapestries represented the lives of St. Peter and St. Paul and were executed in brilliant colors. They were delivered to the chapel between the years 1519 and 1521.

During the sack of Rome in 1527, the tapestries were damaged and two were stolen. They were later recovered and repaired. Some accounts say that the tapestries were seized and put up for auction during the French Revolution when the French invaded Rome. They disappeared until 1808, when they were mysteriously returned to the Vatican. They were restored in 1815, and although not on display in the chapel, they are preserved in the eighth room of the Vatican gallery. In *The Frescoes in the Sistine Chapel*, author Evelyn March Phillips quotes a diarist from Raphael's time who describes the sheer beauty of the tapestries: "The whole chapel was struck dumb by the sight of these hangings; by universal consent there is nothing more beautiful in the world; they are each worth 2000 ducats." Records indicate that Raphael was paid fifteen hundred ducats each for these masterpieces.

St. Peter Healing the Paralytic, *one of the tapestries designed by Raphael for the Sistine Chapel.*

used. Gilding was most often applied to highlight clothing. In the pope's chapel, however, gold highlights also appear in abundance on trees and even on buildings—to breathtaking effect.

THE PAPAL PORTRAITS

The thirty-two papal portraits in the niches above the narrative panels were executed with equal care. Art historians believe that the artists who painted the side panels were responsible for the papal portraits located directly above their own frescoes, although no known records exist to verify this. Each pope wears a ceremonial gown, and a scalloped shell design is painted above his head. Each pose varies, with careful attention paid to the detailed features of the popes' faces. In those instances in which a portrait existed for a pope, the painter tried to follow the drawing to capture the likeness of the pope. When no portrait existed, the rendering of the pope sprang from the mind of the painter.

COMPLETION

The entire project, including wall frescoes, faux draperies, and papal portraits, was completed within two years—no small feat given the scope of the work and the number of artists involved. Pope Sixtus consecrated the frescoes on August 25, 1483, the anniversary of his coronation. The beauty of the frescoes and the decorative work was widely praised upon the opening of the chapel.

The pope was pleased with the execution and grandeur of the finished artwork, but he had little time to enjoy it. Sixtus died in 1484, only one year after the Sistine Chapel was completed. He was buried in the lower level of the chapel, a few yards from the Presepio. His role in the building of the Sistine Chapel had ended, but there was so much more to come.

MICHELANGELO AND THE SISTINE CHAPEL CEILING

The painting of the ceiling by the great artist Michelangelo is the most famous chapter in the chapel's long history. It is one of the largest, most complex, and finest ceiling frescoes in existence. The monumental project, which took four years to complete, garnered far-reaching fame for both the artist and the chapel. Its effect on the art world was immediate and unending. Michelangelo's frescoes are still studied today for their beauty and incomparable mastery of the human form.

Michelangelo's biblical interpretations continued the tradition of using art to emphasize religious beliefs. Yet his design also departed from tradition by including common people in the depiction of religious themes. In this way, Michelangelo glorified not only God but also humankind. While a congregation gazed up at his frecoes, they would learn church doctrine and also feel a part of the miraculous world the artist rendered.

THE POPE COMMISSIONS A NEW WORK

The painting of the great chapel ceiling came to fruition at the insistence of one man: Pope Julius II. Julius, the nephew of Pope Sixtus, was a great patron of the arts. He wished to improve upon his uncle's chapel as well as leave his own mark. He determined that the ceiling should be painted in a grand modern fashion representative of Renaissance tastes and style. For this, he turned to the artist Michelangelo Buonarroti, known throughout Italy and elsewhere in Europe as a superb sculptor, gifted in expressing feelings and emotion through physical forms. His sculptures, *David* in Florence and *The Pietà* in Rome, established his technical expertise and his unique ability to carve emotionally compelling human figures.

Julius had long admired Michelangelo's work. When Julius had decided to build his own tomb, Michelangelo had submitted a design that greatly pleased the pope. The huge tomb, which would measure twenty-four feet wide by thirty-six feet deep and rise almost thirty feet into the air, was to include forty life-size marble statues. Michelangelo had just begun work on the tomb when Julius approached him with the idea of painting the Sistine Chapel ceiling.

The artist at first refused the pope's offer. He saw himself as a sculptor, not a painter. He could not imagine success in so massive an undertaking as the enormous fresco that the pope wished for the ceiling. Like many artists of his day, Michelangelo had learned the art of fresco as a student, but he had little practical experience in it. He could envision only failure, an outcome he believed was the goal of his longtime rival Donato Bramante.

Pope Julius II (pictured) commissioned Michelangelo, whose work he greatly admired, to paint the ceiling of the chapel.

DONATO BRAMANTE

Donato Bramante is considered the founder of the High Renaissance style of architecture, which is known for its reshaping of classical forms to fit more modern needs. He began his artistic career as a painter and often worked on architectural murals. He was also known as a poet and an amateur musician.

Around 1477 Bramante settled in northern Italy near the province of Lombardy, where he began drawing architectural designs. The first structure attributed to him is a church built in Milan. During this time, he often worked closely with his friend Leonardo da Vinci.

Bramante moved to Rome in about 1499 and rapidly rose to prominence, garnering many commissions. His most famous work was the design for St. Peter's Basilica, a huge church incomparable to any other architectural structure on earth. Bramante died in 1514, before the massive structure was completed. After his death, the work was continued by others, including Raphael; Giuliano da Sangallo; Giuliano's nephew, Antonio da Sangallo; and Bramante's rival, Michelangelo. Ironically, St. Peter's famous dome, its most recognizable feature, was designed by Michelangelo.

Michelangelo believed Bramante was behind the pope's request. Bramante, who was the pope's chief architect for a time, knew Michelangelo was inexperienced in fresco. Michelangelo thought this was Bramante's way of damaging his career and thereby advancing the career of Bramante's relative, a young painter from Florence named Raphael. "Bramante wants to prevent me from sculpting, an art at which I am perfect," Michelangelo said. "He wants to force me to paint in fresco, so that everyone will see that I paint worse than his friend Raphael."[7]

Julius, who was unaccustomed to being challenged once he made a decision, rejected the artist's plea to allow him to continue on the tomb. Julius ordered work on the tomb postponed until Michelangelo had completed the painting of the ceiling. Having little choice, the artist accepted the commission in 1508. At the time, he was thirty-three years old and was facing a daunting project. The ceiling, flattened barrel vault measuring 133 feet by 44 feet, was the first ceiling of such large dimensions ever to be decorated in fresco.

THE DESIGN OF THE CEILING

The pope's original idea called for a simple depiction of the Twelve Apostles in the lunettes, the spaces where the walls and ceiling vault meet. The center of the ceiling would be filled in with decorative work. Michelangelo thought the design would turn out poorly and presented a new plan featuring 343 figures framed by painted architectural elements such as faux wood beams and faux marble columns. Years later, in a 1524 letter to his friend Fattucci, Michelangelo expressed the reasoning behind his proposal:

> Having begun the said work it seemed to me it would work out but a poor thing and I told the Pope that by painting only the Apostles there I thought the result would be poor. . . . Then he commissioned me anew that I should do what I wanted."[8]

Michelangelo's ambitious concept for the ceiling featured nine main panels, each representing a scene from the Book of Genesis. These panels included: *God Separating Light from Darkness; The Creation of the Sun, Moon, and Stars; The Separation of Land from Water; The Creation of Adam; The Creation of Eve; The Temptation and Fall of Adam; The Sacrifice of Noah; The Flood;* and *The Drunkenness of Noah.* The first four frescoes—representing the fall of humanity—were positioned over the front half of the chapel, where the congregation and laymen would sit. The last five frescoes—representing the history of God—were positioned over the half of the chapel containing the presbytery, or the part reserved for the clergy. The panels vary in size, creating a sense of movement throughout the center of the

Donato Bramante, founder of the High Renaissance architectural style and rival of Michelangelo.

The Creation of Adam *depicts God (right) giving life to Adam with a touch of his finger.*

ceiling. This would not have been the case had all of the panels been exactly the same size.

The sibyls and prophets, soothsayers representing man's belief in divinely inspired messengers, line each side of the scenes from Genesis. The lunettes over the windows consist of common people involved in everyday activity. Scattered throughout the frecoes are Ignudi—nude spiritual beings caught between humankind and divinity—holding garlands of oak leaves and acorns, which were ancient Roman symbols of eternal life and were associated with the della Rovere family. The ceiling also features numerous cupids and small bronze medallions relating bible stories.

Michelangelo also proposed including the curved areas where the wall and ceiling meet as part of the ceiling design. All scenes are sectioned off and framed by painted marble and limestone architectural work resembling beams and columns. These illusionary architectural elements provide viewers with the sense of viewing a three-dimensional structure. So columns appear to thicken toward the walls in response to the weight, outward thrust, and downward pressure that would naturally be present.

Revolutionary in many respects, Michelangelo departed from traditional Christian art by deliberately painting saints without halos or wings and God without a crown. Still, the entire design, which is overwhelming in scope and size, represents the basic Christian belief in a preordained history of unfolding events following a divine plan.

The pope approved the new design, and the project went forward. Records indicate that Michelangelo was to be paid six thousand ducats, a fair amount of money for the time period but not a lot for the complexity of the work itself.

THE SCAFFOLDING

To execute the monumental task, Michelangelo first had to construct scaffolding able to reach the eighty-seven-foot-high ceiling.

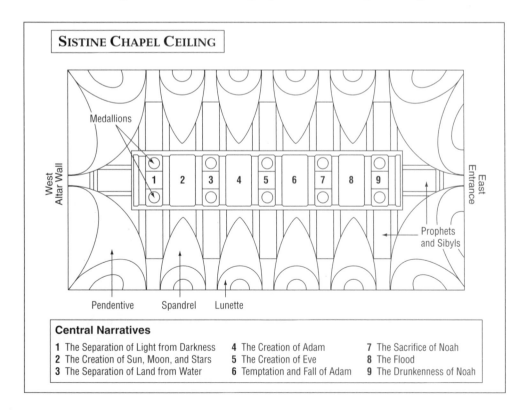

SISTINE CHAPEL CEILING

Medallions

West Altar Wall

East Entrance

1 2 3 4 5 6 7 8 9

Prophets and Sibyls

Pendentive   Spandrel   Lunette

Central Narratives

1 The Separation of Light from Darkness
2 The Creation of Sun, Moon, and Stars
3 The Separation of Land from Water
4 The Creation of Adam
5 The Creation of Eve
6 Temptation and Fall of Adam
7 The Sacrifice of Noah
8 The Flood
9 The Drunkenness of Noah

MICHELANGELO'S SCAFFOLDING

Michelangelo's scaffolding for the ceiling project in the Sistine Chapel was a masterpiece in design. The artist proved that his architectural talents were equal to his sculpture and painting skills. The scaffolding was portable, with portions that could be removed to view the ceiling from below and judge the effect from the floor. The scaffolding consisted of an arched bridge with a large center platform for painting the middle of the vault. In addition, side steps followed the curve of the vault and allowed the artist to work on the rounded sections and on the lunettes on the vertical surfaces of the walls. The bridge was constructed so that it actually gained strength once any weight was placed on it. The entire structure was supported by a huge wooden beam that spanned the entire space and rested on wooden brackets attached to the side walls. A series of six oblong holes, one over each pair of windows, allowed the complete structure to be moved as the painting progressed. The positions of the holes mirror the painted architecture of the ceiling.

The scaffolding needed to be left in place as the work progressed yet allow the chapel to remain open.

The scaffolding design conceived by Bramante caused immediate problems. Bramante's scaffold was to be suspended from the ceiling by a series of ropes. Michelangelo disliked this design because it would leave holes in the artwork once the scaffolding was removed. Bramante could not satisfactorily answer how the holes would be later filled. Michelangelo, a master architect in his own right, then obtained permission from the pope to design his own scaffolding. His system would be in the form of an arch, with platforms erected from the floor of the chapel. This design allowed Michelangelo to paint while standing and to freely move around while he worked the pigments into the fresco before it dried. Though this stance proved most uncomfortable because it required continual craning of the neck, it offered the artist the mobility and perspective he required. The scaffolding was successfully constructed by May 1508, and Michelangelo began his work.

MICHELANGELO AND THE GARZONI

Although Michelangelo prefered to work alone, he was assigned a number of *garzoni,* or assistants, to help with the work. A perfectionist with a volatile temper, Michelangelo found his assistants' skills lacking and felt their work did not harmonize with his own. By October 7, 1508, he had fired one assistant; shortly thereafter the other four were locked out of the chapel, presumably by Michelangelo. Historian Giorgio Vasari gives this version of events:

> Michelangelo caused them [the *garzoni*] to paint a portion by way of specimen, but what they had done was far from approaching his expectations or fulfilling his purpose, and one morning he determined to destroy the whole of it. He then shut himself up in the chapel, and not only would he never again permit the building to be opened to them, but he likewise refused to see any one of them at his house. Finally therefore, and when the jest appeared to them to be carried too far, they returned, ashamed and mortified, to Florence. Michelangelo then made arrangements for performing the whole work himself, sparing no care nor labor, in the hope of bringing the same to a satisfactory termination.[9]

Eventually Michelangelo did acquire a group of *garzoni* with whom he could work. Surviving records list several artists who worked on the vault: Piero Rosselli, who applied the plaster; Granacci; Aristotele Guiliano Bugiardini; Agnolo d. Donnino; Iacopo d. Sandro (who was later replaced by Indaco Vecchio); and Giovanni Michi, a handyman. These men worked in a very controlled environment, strictly supervised by Michelangelo. Because of the master artist's exacting standards, the *garzoni* were reduced to supporting tasks such as grinding colors, applying plaster, tracing the cartoons and pouncing, and executing decorative painting with Michelangelo often finishing portions begun by others. Several decorative portions of the frescoes clearly show the work of at least six different artists. The brush strokes vary widely and do not match Michelangelo's.

THE PAINTING OF THE CEILING

After receiving his first payment of five hundred ducats, Michelangelo began work on the frescoes on May 10, 1508. Using nails,

Historians believe The Flood *was the first of the nine ceiling frescoes that Michelangelo worked on.*

cords, and rulers, he arranged the architectural designs and ornamental emblems. (One of the original nails used to fasten a cartoon to the ceiling is still embedded near the figure of Ezekiel.) The first panel he worked on was most likely *The Flood.* That panel shows evidence of being reworked at some point, probably once Michelangelo gained more experience with fresco.

Shortly after finishing the panel, the artist noticed mold on the fresco. The mold may have resulted from high humidity or problems with the plaster mixture. That mixture, consisting of Roman lime and volcanic dust, dried slowly, often causing salt within the mixture to effloresce, or change to a powdery crust. The artist despaired. When the pope visited to view the progress, Michelangelo did not recognize him. The enraged artist rushed at Julius with a plank of wood from the scaffolding, trying to drive him out of the chapel. Upon realizing who the intruder was, Michelangelo apologized and helped the pope climb the scaffolding to inspect the work. The pope assumed the mold problem could be resolved and urged Michelangelo to continue painting.

One of Michelangelo's friends, the noted architect and sculptor Giuliano da Sangallo, was called in for consultation.

MOLD ON THE MASTERPIECE

Historian Giorgio Vasari, as quoted in Pierluigi de Vecchi's *The Sistine Chapel: A Glorious Restoration*, discusses the mold that started to grow on the ceiling of the chapel after Michelangelo began his work.

When he had completed about one-third of the painting, the prevalence of the north wind during the winter months had caused a sort of mould [mold] to appear on the pictures; and this happened from the fact that in Rome, the plaster, made of travertine and puzzolana, does not dry rapidly, and while in a soft state is somewhat dark and very fluent, not to say watery; when the wall is covered with this mixture, therefore, it throws out an efflorescence arising from the humid saltiness which bursts forth; but this is in time evaporated and corrected by the air. Michelangelo was, indeed in despair at the sight of these spots, and refused to continue the work, declaring to the Pope that he could not succeed therein, but His Holiness sent Giuliano da Sangallo to look at it, and he, telling the artist whence these spots arose, encouraged him to proceed, by teaching him how they might be removed.

Sangallo determined the mold was caused by the efflorescence of the natural salt in the fresco mixture and by the humidity present in the chapel. He showed Michelangelo how to prevent the mold from growing.

MICHELANGELO'S SKILL AND MASTERY GROWS

In a short time, Michelangelo became adept at the technique of fresco. He could cover an area approximately forty-three square feet in one day. He worked quickly, drawing the necessary cartoons using huge quantities of costly paper. Any cartoons not ruined during the transfer process were given away to friends and were subsequently lost; Michelangelo ordered the few remaining cartoons in his possession to be burned in 1517.

The first half of the ceiling was done with the pouncing technique. The second half used both pouncing and incision, possibly because Michelangelo desired to work more and more quickly to complete the project. He also sometimes sketched directly onto the ceiling using sinopia, a red ochre named after Sinope, a town on the Black Sea known for its red pigments.

Michelangelo often referred to the chapel as "the barn." Working above the window level with the scaffolding blocking off much of the natural light coming from below, Michelangelo probably was forced to use candles. He applied the pigments in a series of distinctive, closely spaced brush strokes, choosing very bright colors to compensate for the dimness of the chapel. His color palette was not large, but it was brilliantly luminous. He varied the thickness of the paint, applying it in layers to create a beautiful translucent effect much like watercolors. Softer colors dominate the large areas, with brilliant accents used in smaller portions of the frescoes. As the work progressed, the colors became slightly more muted, suggesting a change in the artist's style.

Michelangelo was also quite skilled at incorporating chiaroscuro—that is, the interplay of light and shade without regard to color. Through his deft use of light and shadow, figures emerge from the ceiling as though they were sculptures come to life. Very little landscape was used in the panels so as not to draw focus from the figures.

After the first three frescoes were completed, Michelangelo viewed them from the floor and determined that the figures were too small. His figures became noticeably larger as he worked toward the altar. The figures also became more powerful and fewer in number. Perhaps the artist intentionally wished to compensate for the great distance from the entrance to the altar. Although dissimilar in size, the larger figures harmonize with the smaller ones when viewed from the entrance. Patches of sky within the scenes of the larger and smaller panels pull the scenes together and add a celestial feel to the entire vault.

A MAN OBSESSED

Michelangelo worked at an inhuman pace, as was his habit. He took few breaks for meals or sleep, as described in Ascanio Condivi's 1533 biography of the artist:

> He was always very frugal in his lifestyle, eating more out of necessity than enjoyment, especially when working,

Michelangelo's figures became larger and more powerful as he worked toward the altar, as seen in The Creation of the Sun, Moon, and Stars.

AN IMPORTANT AND ENDURING ARTIST

Michelangelo Buonarroti was not only a great sculptor and painter, but also an accomplished poet and architect. Born in 1475 in the small village of Caprese, he was sent to Florence at the age of thirteen to study in the studio of the fresco master Ghirlandajo. Soon the prominent art patron Lorenzo de' Medici invited Michelangelo to stay in his household. The artist's tremendous talent was obvious early in his life. He produced at least two marble relief sculptures at the age of sixteen. His most famous sculptures, *The Pietà* (depicting the Virgin Mary holding a dying Jesus across her lap) in St. Peter's Basilica and the giant statue of *David* in Florence, were both executed before the artist was thirty years old.

Michelangelo also proved his skill as a painter with the huge frescoes he completed in the Sistine Chapel. The works depict biblical stories and cover fifty-six hundred square feet on the ceiling and altar wall.

As an architect, his crowning achievement was the dome of St. Peter's Basilica, which became a model for domes all over the world. In fact, the dome of the Capitol building in Washington, D.C., is derived from Michelangelo's design.

He died in 1564 in Rome, leaving a legacy of artistic achievements that still inspire the world today.

Michelangelo Buonarroti, one of the most accomplished Renaissance artists.

and at these times he has been happy with a piece of bread, eating it while working. . . . And just as he has eaten little food, so he has slept little. According to him sleep gives him a headache and too much sleep gives him indigestion. When he was stronger, he often slept with all his clothes on and his breeches on his legs, which he wears for cramps which has always bothered him. Sometimes he has left his breeches on so long that when he has removed them, the skin has come off too, like a snake.[10]

By August 1510, he had completed most of the first half of the ceiling. The difficult labor of the project was not Michelangelo's only problem, though. Conflict over receiving payments from the pope also troubled him. In a letter to his family, who had been urging him to come to Florence for a visit, Michelangelo expressed his inability to make the journey due to financial problems: "The 500 ducats I have earned under the agreement are due to me, and as much again which the Pope must give me to start the rest of the work. But he has gone away and left me no instructions, and so I find myself without money and do not know what I should do."[11]

Pope Julius had his own difficulties. During this time, rebels had captured the city of Bologna, and the pope left Rome to lead an army against them. He was occupied with this war for several months and was ultimately victorious. Upon his triumphant return to Rome, he learned that Michelangelo had done no work on the ceiling. Angered, he ordered that the artist take up his brushes immediately. Coming to a financial agreement with the pope, Michelangelo began more frescoes in January 1511.

THE SCAFFOLDING IS TEMPORARILY REMOVED

The following August, Pope Julius ordered the removal of the scaffolding in time for the August 15 Feast of the Assumption mass celebrating the Virgin Mary's journey to the kingdom of heaven. This presented Michelangelo with his first opportunity to view his work without obstruction. A stylistic change is evident in the remaining half of the ceiling, toward the altar. Not only are the figures larger, but the frescoes also seem to have been executed in a more confident manner. Their scope and power are magnificent. The nudes also feature more torsion, or an intense twisting of the body, which Michelangelo favored in his work as a means of emphasizing the beauty of the human form.

By this time, Pope Julius, who was nearly seventy years old and was in poor health, had grown anxious about seeing the finished ceiling. The work had thus far taken three years, and the pope's impatience was increasing. He often stopped by the chapel to view the painting and to remind the painter of his duty to finish before age or illness deprived the pope of the pleasure of seeing the finished work. Historian Vasari describes one heated exchange between the pope and the artist, in which the two men parry over the pace of the work. Vasari writes,

> His Holiness was always asking him importunately when it would be ready. . . . [Michelangelo] retorted that the ceiling would be finished "when it satisfies me as an artist . . . " And to this the Pope replied, "And we want you to satisfy us and finish it soon." Finally, the Pope threatened that if Michelangelo did not finish the ceiling quickly he would have him thrown down from the scaffolding.[12]

THE LUNETTES

Michelangelo painted the lunettes last, starting them in 1511. They were similar in scale to the frescoes on the side walls and served as a transition to the larger panels and figures of the vault. The lunettes, painted on the vertical surface directly be-

Pope Julius II often checked on Michelangelo's progress as he grew impatient with the artist's pace.

low the curve of the vault, were accessed by the stepped sides of the scaffolding. Michelangelo most likely began work on the lunettes on the south wall, where the natural light was dimmer and would hide any initial errors.

The lunettes show no evidence of either pouncing or incision, and it appears that Michelangelo executed the paintings directly on the surface without the aid of cartoons to guide him. He worked quickly; the *giornates* for each lunette indicate only three days' work or less. Michelangelo painted with a furious compulsion, actually leaving brush hairs embedded in the frescoes. In less than one year's time, he painted a total of fourteen lunettes in the semicircular areas above the existing papal portraits.

Letters from Michelangelo speak of his weariness and overexertion at this time. In addition to exhaustion, he experienced constant back and neck pain and increasingly poor eyesight. In a letter dated July 24, 1512, he stated, "I struggle more than any man ever has, in bad health and with the greatest labor, and still I remain patient in order to reach the desired goal."[13]

A letter to his brother, Buonarroto, on the same date again stresses his confidence in his ability to complete the work despite his poor physical health:

> I have not time to reply to your letter because it is night, and even if I did have time I do not know how my affairs will end here. . . . I work more than any man ever did, in ill health and in the greatest discomfort; but I still have the endurance to achieve the end I long for.[14]

One month later, in a letter to his brother dated August 21, it is apparent that Michelangelo's family had been pressuring him to complete his task and return to Florence:

> I have had your letter, and I'm replying briefly for lack of time. As for my returning there [to Florence], I cannot return until I finish the work, which I reckon to finish by the end of September; but truly the labour is so immense that I cannot say within a fortnight. Enough to say that I'll be there before All Saints by all means. I am hurrying as much as I can, because it seems a thousand years till I'm home.[15]

"BENT AS BOWMEN BEND A BOW"

Michelangelo wrote a humorous sonnet to his friend Giovanni da Pistoia about the toll the painting of the Sistine Chapel ceiling was taking on his body. The poem is recorded in *Michelangelo, a Self Portrait*, edited by Robert J. Clements.

> In this hard toil I've such a goiter grown,
> Like cats that water drink in Lombardy,
> (Or wheresoever else the place may be)
> That chin and belly meet perforce in one.
> My beard doth point to heaven, my scalp its place
> Upon my shoulder finds; my chest, you'll say,
> A harpy's is, my paint-brush all the day
> Doth drop a rich mosaic on my face.
> My loins have entered my paunch within,
> My nether end my balance doth supply.
> My feet unseen move to and fro in vain.
> In front to utmost length is stretched my skin
> And wrinkled up in folds behind, while I
> Am bent as bowmen bend a bow in Spain.
> No longer true or sane,
> The judgment now doth from the mind proceed,
> For 'tis ill shooting through a twisted reed.
> Then thou, my picture dead,
> Defend it, Giovan, and my honor—why?
> The place is wrong, and no painter I.

He even wrote a sonnet to his friend Giovanni da Pistoia describing how bent and unnatural his posture had become as a result of constantly working on the chapel's scaffolding. He suffered the physical effects of this prolonged position for many years, as noted in Ascanio Condivi's biography of Michelangelo:

> After finishing this work, because of having painted for so long with his eyes raised towards the vault, he could see very little looking downwards, so that if he had to read a letter or look at very small things, he had to hold them over his head with his arms.[16]

By October 31, 1512, Michelangelo had finally finished his work, and he sent a short note to his father: "I've finished that chapel I was painting. The Pope is quite satisfied."[17]

THE FINISHED CEILING IS REVEALED

Pope Julius was indeed pleased, and he had the scaffolding quickly disassembled so the ceiling could be revealed to the public on All Saint's Day, November 1. All who viewed the masterpiece lauded it. The master sculptor had become a master painter. Michelangelo was the recipient of high praise from the public, including Vasari:

> The ceiling has proved a veritable beacon to our art, of inestimable benefit to all painters, restoring light to a world that for centuries had been plunged into darkness. . . . In

Michelangelo's finished ceiling was exhibited in 1512 and earned accolades from the pope and the public.

the nudes, Michelangelo displayed complete mastery: they are truly astonishing in their perfect foreshortenings, their wonderfully rotund contours, their grace, slenderness, and proportion.[18]

The only criticism Michelangelo received concerned the ceiling's lack of gilding, which was prominent in frescoes of the time. The pope later urged him to reassemble the scaffolding and add gold touches to the frescoes, saying they would be enriched by them. To this, Michelangelo replied: "Holy Father, the figures I painted show poor folk and holy men, who despised riches and ornament."[19] The ceiling remained as it was.

Pope Julius did not long enjoy the realization of his dream; he died in February 1513. The masterpiece that Michelangelo had created during his four years of unprecedented labor remains unsurpassed in its scope and artistic execution. In many ways, the Sistine Chapel epitomizes the Renaissance movement. As with much of Renaissance art, its grandeur was inspired by classical compositions yet developed by Michelangelo in new and modern ways.

Further praise from Vasari declares the futility of any other artist's attempt to match what Michelangelo accomplished with the frescoes of the chapel:

No painter need concern himself with new attitudes, new methods with drapery, new ways of expressing the wonderful and the terrible in art. You have only to look at a face painted by Michelangelo to see every conceivable perfection.[20]

THE LAST JUDGMENT

The Last Judgment is the largest single wall fresco executed during the Renaissance period. It encompasses 2,475 square feet and contains over four hundred human figures. The fresco depicts the church's belief in resurrection, which is death followed by either redemption and ascension to heaven or damnation and descent to hell. Its placement on the altar wall, in the most prominent spot in the chapel, reflects the importance of this idea in Christianity. The constant reminder of Jesus as savior is visible to all. The use of art to emphasize religious beliefs can be no more evident than the placement and theme of this huge fresco in the pope's own chapel.

Pope Clement VII, who headed the church from 1523 to 1534, wished to leave his own mark on the Sistine Chapel. He chose for his legacy a depiction of the Last Judgment. The scene was to be painted on the altar wall and above the main door of the chapel. In order to accomplish this, several existing frescoes had to be destroyed. Historians believe Pope Clement wished to have *The Last Judgment* prominently displayed to serve as a commemoration that he and the church were delivered from enemies during the sack of Rome in May 1527. It was a time of great political upheaval; German, Spanish, and Italian troops under the banner of the Holy Roman Emperor invaded the city and plundered, tortured, raped, and murdered the citizens. The Sistine Chapel and its treasures were spared.

The pope's first choice of an artist for the project was Sebastiano del Piombo, who proposed the work be done in oils. Instead, the pope decided that he wanted Michelangelo to do the work in fresco, possibly to continue the harmony of the artwork as a whole. Michelangelo was the obvious best choice to design and execute new frescoes that would complement his previous masterpiece on the ceiling.

In 1533 Pope Clement traveled to Florence to convince Michelangelo to accept the commission. According to Giorgio Vasari, the pope's wishes were discussed in detail in a meeting between the two on September 22:

Pope Clement VII commissioned Michelangelo to paint The Last Judgment *in 1533.*

On the main (facade) where the altar is, [Clement suggested that Michelangelo] should paint the Last Judgment so that he could show in the story everything that the art of drawing could achieve: and that on the opposite wall, above the main door, he ordered him to do so to show when because of his pride Lucifer was expelled from heaven and cast down into the centre of hell with all those angels who sinned with him.[21]

Michelangelo, who was happy with the work he was already engaged in, was once again reluctant to accept a commission that would require him to return to Rome. Pressure from Pope Clement eventually persuaded the artist to agree to the project, and Michelangelo began a series of cartoons for *The Last Judgment.*

POPE PAUL III SUCCEEDS POPE CLEMENT

Pope Clement died shortly after Michelangelo began his preliminary drawings, and Pope Paul III was elected his successor. Michelangelo hoped to be excused from his agreement so that he could continue his work in Florence. Pope Paul, who also wished to beautify the chapel, was pleased with the cartoons in progress and wanted Michelangelo to continue his project. Michelangelo tried to appeal to the new pope, saying he had a contract previously established with the duke of Urbino. The pope, angered, exclaimed, "I have wanted this for thirty years and now that I am Pope will you not satisfy me? I shall tear up the contract [with Urbino] and I am prepared for you to serve me in every way."[22] Michelangelo relented. A letter pertaining to the plans dated February 20, 1534, states that the pope "has managed to persuade Michelangelo to paint in the Chapel and so above the altar there will be the Resurrection, for which the scaffolding is already prepared."[23]

To further bind Michelangelo to his service, Pope Paul named the artist papal architect, granting him a life stipend in the enormous sum of twelve hundred gold crowns a year.

PREPARATIONS BEGIN

The preparation for the fresco that would be entitled *The Last Judgment* was time consuming. It took several months to demolish existing work, including an altarpiece, two of Michelangelo's own ceiling lunettes, and two frescoes by Perugino, *The Nativity* and *The Finding of Moses*. Spaces on either side of the altar, which were specifically designed to house two of Raphael's famous tapestries, were also lost. These tapestries depicted the lives of St. Peter and St. Paul.

The two windows behind the altar were filled in, and the entire wall was rebricked and reconstructed so that it jutted out slightly from the top to help keep the dust from settling on the altar. Keeping the chapel and its artwork clean was an

POPE PAUL III

Pope Paul III was descended from the Farnese, an ancient Roman family of aristocrats. He was given the best education available and moved in exclusive social circles, forming a strong friendship with Leo X, who was also destined to become a pope.

Before being named pope, Paul rose rapidly through the ranks of the clergy. In 1534, when he was sixty-six years old, he was named successor to Clement VII. He was responsible for forming the Council of Trent in 1545, which was in charge of strengthening and reforming the Catholic Church. This council became the cornerstone of the Counter Reformation movement. Pope Paul was a commanding presence and a man absolutely dedicated to saving his church. His efforts, along with the council's energetic actions, established for all times the fundamental truths of the Catholic doctrine on the Scriptures, original sin, justification, and the Sacraments.

When the pope died at the age of eighty-two, he was buried in St. Peter's Basilica in a tomb designed by Michelangelo. His remarkable personality and dedication is credited with turning the tide in favor of his beloved religion during the most trying times in the history of the Catholic Church.

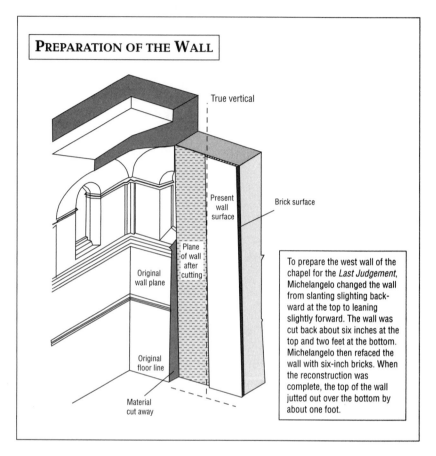

PREPARATION OF THE WALL

True vertical

Present wall surface

Brick surface

Plane of wall after cutting

Original wall plane

Original floor line

Material cut away

To prepare the west wall of the chapel for the *Last Judgement*, Michelangelo changed the wall from slanting slighting backward at the top to leaning slightly forward. The wall was cut back about six inches at the top and two feet at the bottom. Michelangelo then refaced the wall with six-inch bricks. When the reconstruction was complete, the top of the wall jutted out over the bottom by about one foot.

ongoing problem. The angling of the wall was insisted upon by Michelangelo, and it was built according to his strict specifications. Then the wall had to be plastered and prepared to receive the fresco.

Sebastiano del Piombo was in charge of surfacing the wall. During this time, an argument broke out between Michelangelo and Sebastiano over the choice of plaster and application technique that had been used. A three-month delay occurred between January and March 1536 when Sebastiano's surface was removed and then replaced by the surface Michelangelo required.

When Michelangelo was finally ready to apply the first pigments, more than three years had passed since his original agreement with Pope Clement. He began the fresco in the summer of 1536.

MICHELANGELO'S STYLE AND TECHNIQUE

Michelangelo painted from the top of the fresco toward the bottom, lowering the scaffolding as he progressed. Cartoons were used on nearly all of the figures, which were transferred by the pouncing technique in the majority of instances. But as with the ceiling, when the artist neared the end of his labor and was perhaps anxious to complete it, he utilized both pouncing and the much faster incising technique evident in the lower portions of *The Last Judgment*, mostly in the figures of the demons.

His color palette, which was more subdued than the brilliant hues of the ceiling, consisted of about a dozen shades. Michelangelo used many earthy colors and flesh tones as well as large quantities of the expensive lapis lazuli for the large expanse of sky. He applied the paint in a much heavier manner than the delicate layering of the ceiling pigments, which gave a depth and consistency to the flesh of the figures.

Some of the pigments he chose, such as lacquer; *giallolino;* and orpiment, an orange or yellow pigment, could only be used *a secco*. He also made some corrections in *a secco* as well as executed a few small figures that have since faded.

As before, Michelangelo was consumed by his art and worked at an extraordinary pace. But if not for the insistence of a surgeon friend, Baccio Rontini, Michelangelo would not even have sought treatment after suffering from a fall off the scaffolding. His leg was injured, and Rontini forced him to accept medical attention. Michelangelo recovered quickly and returned to the chapel, laboring continuously in order to finish.

Records indicate that Michelangelo had only one assistant for *The Last Judgment,* a talented artist named Urbino. Among his many abilities, Urbino excelled at the technique of foreshortening. Foreshortening requires the artist to literally shorten details in the painting in order to give the figures depth. Foreshortening on *The Last Judgment*, a flat wall viewed in close proximity, presented a different challenge than on the vault of the ceiling, which was viewed from a much greater distance. On December 15, 1540, the scaffolding was lowered to uncover the finished upper portion of the fresco. Historians speculate that Michelangelo and his assistant took this opportunity to correct problems with foreshortening.

MICHELANGELO'S TENACITY

Michelangelo's tenacity and stubborn nature, even when sustaining personal injury during the painting of *The Last Judgment*, was recorded by historian Giorgio Vasari and recounted in Fabrizio Mancinelli's *The Sistine Chapel*.

> Towards the end of the undertaking there was also an accident: Michelangelo fell from the scaffolding and hurt his leg, but initially "in the pain and the anger (sic) this caused him" he refused medical attention. Tended by force by his surgeon friend Baccio Rontini he recovered quickly and "having returned to his work, he labored continuously for some months when he brought it to an end, giving so much force to the figures that they verified the description of Dante: "Dead are the dead, the living seem to live"; the sufferings of the damned and the joys of the blessed are exhibited with equal truth.

THE DESIGN OF *THE LAST JUDGMENT*

Even before work on *The Last Judgment* was completed, it was clear to many who saw it that it was a masterpiece. Michelangelo's maturity as an artist (he was now sixty-one years old) shows in his total and incomparable mastery of the human figure. As historian Evelyn March Phillips expresses,

> the drawing of all these forms in every attitude is a perpetual study of limb and muscle, of foreshortening and movement, and of scale of size. The whole shows a knowledge of anatomy, of values, of effect and grouping which is almost overpowering.[24]

The multitude of figures span the huge wall in a circular configuration with no architectural elements (such as the faux columns of the ceiling). The uppermost part of the fresco represents Paradise, with two groups of wingless angels in the spaces where the lunettes previously were. These angels bear the cross, a crown of thorns, the pillar of Scourging, and other instruments of the Passion of Christ. In the center, Christ the Judge rises from a throne of clouds with his mother, the Virgin Mary, at his side. They are surrounded by saints, apostles, prophets, and patriarchs who await Christ's pronouncement. On the left side of the painting, the saved souls are struggling to emerge from the earth, some as skeletons still without flesh. On the right side, the damned souls are being cast into Hell by angels and demons, twisted in grotesque positions, their terrible expressions conveying deep spiritual anguish.

The Last Judgment depicts Christ, in the center with his arm raised, judging humanity.

This detail from the lower right corner of The Last Judgment *shows the charon, a mythological creature who ferried the dead to the underworld, forcing the souls of the damned to depart into Hell.*

Many experts in art and literature have suggested that inspiration for Michelangelo's depiction of Heaven and Hell came from *The Divine Comedy*, written by the Italian poet Dante in 1321. One of the most important Christian poems ever written, it describes an imaginary journey through Heaven and Hell. In the lower right corner of *The Last Judgment*, Michelangelo depicts a mythological spirit called a charon standing in a boat with an oar raised against the damned, forcing them to disembark. The scene coincides with Dante's narrative: "Charon, the spirit with eyes of fire, has gathered them all together with a sign, fells with his oar any who still hesitate."[25]

Minossis, who has a serpent wrapped around his body and the ears of an ass springing from his head, welcomes the damned to the threshold of Hell. Minossis and the charon, both mythical creatures from Dante's writings, are the only two exceptions to the otherwise strictly biblical depictions in *The Last Judgment*.

SELF-PORTRAITS

Other interesting aspects of *The Last Judgment* are the self-portraits Michelangelo included. In the first self-portrait, located on the bottom left of the fresco, he has depicted himself as an old man helping the saved souls rise from the dead. The second and most well-known self-portrait is a haunting and grotesque rendering of his face on the flayed skin of a man held by the apostle St. Bartholomew. Michelangelo's self-portrait was easily distinguished because he truthfully depicted his crooked nose, which had been broken in a childhood brawl by his friend Piero Torrigiani.

THE CRITICISM BEGINS

Although praise for the artist's work came from from many corners, so did criticism. Nudity, common in artwork of the period,

Michelangelo included two self-portraits in The Last Judgment, *one of which appears in the flayed skin in the lower right corner of this detail.*

MICHELANGELO'S CROOKED NOSE

Michelangelo included many self-portraits in his works, which were easily identified by his crooked nose. In Waldemar Januszczak's *Sayonara, Michelangelo: The Sistine Chapel Restored and Repackaged*, the artist's childhood friend Piero Torrigiani explains how Michelangelo came to have a broken nose.

This [Michelangelo] Buonarroti and I used, when we were boys, to go into the Church of the Carmine, to learn drawing from the Chapel of Masaccio. It was Buonarroti's habit to banter all who were drawing there; and one day, among others, when he was annoying me, I got more angry than usual, and clenching my fist, gave him such a blow on the nose, that I felt bone and cartilage go down like a biscuit beneath my knuckles; and this mark of mine he will carry with him to the grave.

had never been seen in religious art on the scale of what appeared in Michelangelo's *The Last Judgment*. The sight of so many nude figures surrounding Christ incensed many viewers. One of the first to express outrage over all of the naked figures was a member of the papal secretariat, Biago da Cesena, who declared, "That belongs in a bath house and not in the Pope's Chapel. All those nudes, those men and women, are indecent!"[26]

Michelangelo exacted a most unusual revenge when he gave the figure of Satan in his fresco the face of Biago. To add insult to injury, Michelangelo painted a serpent coiling around Satan and biting him on the groin. An enraged Biago rushed to Pope Paul to lodge a formal complaint against Michelangelo. The pope, who was all too familiar with the artist's temper and had already given him complete freedom in the execution of the painting, told Biago, "Only earth, purgatory, and paradise are under my authority; in hell I have no power at all."[27] The painting was not changed.

Michelangelo completed his masterpiece on October 31, 1541. The fresco had taken five years to paint, and Michelangelo was now sixty-six years old. The artist's frescoes now covered fifty-six hundred square feet of the chapel's interior and included more than six hundred human and mythical figures.

When *The Last Judgment* was unveiled, the members of the pontifical court present were overcome with emotions of amazement, delight, and wonder. But some members of the public thought it scandalous, and the fresco's critics were vicious in their response, launching cruel attacks against what they deemed an unholy rendering of a most holy subject. Three weeks after the unveiling, Nino Sernini, a visitor to the chapel, wrote to Cardinal Ercole Gonzaga in defense of *The Last Judgment*. His comments, while clearly stating the controversial aspects, distinctly uphold the masterpiece for its incomparable beauty:

> Although the work is of such beauty as Your Illustrious Lordship may imagine there are indeed those who do not like it . . . [some] say that the nudes are not fitting in such a place, showing their parts, even though Michelangelo has exercised considerable tact in this, and there are scarcely ten in the whole multitude where you can see sexual organs. Others complain that the Christ has no beard and is too young, and hasn't the majesty He should have, and in general there is no shortage of carping, but the Very Reverend Cornaro, who went to study them for a long time, seems to have it right, saying that if Michelangelo were willing to give him in a picture just one of those figures, he would gladly pay him whatever he asked, and I agree, because I do not believe one can see the like of it anywhere else.[28]

The controversy continued for years. Pope Paul IV requested that Michelangelo "mend" the painting, presumably meaning he should cover the nudity. Michelangelo had absolutely no intention of doing so. He sarcastically replied, "Tell His Holiness that this is a mere trifle and can easily be done; let him mend the world, paintings are easily mended."[29]

THE FRESCO IS ALTERED

In January 1564, a few weeks before Michelangelo's death, the decision to alter *The Last Judgment* was taken before the Council of Trent. The council consisted of holy men and church leaders who set church policies. When presented with the problem of *The Last Judgment*, the council agreed that changes should be made. New scaffolding was built by Florentine carpenter Zanobio di Mariotto. In 1565 Daniele da Volterra was chosen to paint clothing over various figures in the fresco. Because of this commission, da Volterra forever earned the nickname "the Breeches Painter."[30]

Before da Volterra painted over the nudity in *The Last Judgment*, Martino Rota made an engraved copy of the original, the only one in existence. Rota was a Yugoslav historian who made copies of many famous artworks during the sixteenth century. His engravings are the only records left of many important works that have since been destroyed by fire, time, or other causes. His engraving of *The Last Judgment* has been an invaluable help to other historians in determining what changes were made.

It is not clear exactly how many figures da Volterra painted. Various drawings made of the fresco during the sixteenth century, after da Volterra's work, show figures without loincloths. Experts believe *The Last Judgment* was painted over as many

DANIELE DA VOLTERRA

Daniele da Volterra, an Italian painter, stuccoist, and sculptor, was born in 1509. He traveled to Rome sometime around 1535 to execute frescoes and stucco work on Cardinal Agostino Trivulzio's private villa, which was situated just outside the city. In Rome, some of his decorative frieze work still remains today. It shows that the artist was influenced by others working during that time such as Raphael and Michelangelo. It is particularly evident that the muscular figures da Volterra painted echo those of Michelangelo's famous ceiling in the Sistine Chapel.

He executed many frescoes for various churches and chapels around Rome. He was also commissioned by Pope Paul III to assist the artist Perino on various projects. After Perino's death in 1547, da Voltera continued the work on his own but lost that privilege after the pope's death in 1549.

Some art scholars say da Volterra's worst work is a mere imitation of those artists he admired, but his best work is inventive and exhibits a refreshing and unusual use of color. His most famous work was commissioned by Pope Paul IV in 1565. Da Volterra died in 1566 after completing the project. His work on *The Last Judgment* unfortunately earned him the nickname "the Breeches Painter," and it forever overshadowed his artistic reputation.

Some church officials objected to the nudity in The Last Judgment *and ordered clothing to be painted over the genitals.*

as four times after its completion. In 1762 author J. Richard, upon visiting the chapel, noted "some very mediocre artists working to cover with draperies the most beautiful nude figures on the wall and on the ceiling."[31]

After centuries of controversy, *The Last Judgment* is now considered to be a masterpiece of Michelangelo's mature painting and an important and beautiful addition to the Sistine Chapel's art treasures. The chapel is also unique because it preserves two of Michelangelo's most famous works from different periods in his life. *The Last Judgment* and the famous ceiling complete the chapel's decoration in a more glorious fashion than could have been imagined when the initial plans were conceived. It has been admired and revered for centuries.

The German poet and playwright Goethe, who gained fame as the author of *Faust*, wrote on December 2, 1786,

> On the 28th [of November] we paid a second visit to the Sistine Chapel. . . . All . . . is fully compensated by the sight of the great masterpiece of art. And at this moment I am so taken with Michelangelo, that after him I have no taste even for nature herself, especially as I am unable to contemplate her with the same eye of genius that he did.[32]

Historic Restorations

The Sistine Chapel weathered time and turmoil remarkably well. The building, as well as the famous frescoes, remained virtually intact over the centuries, with one small exception: On June 28, 1797, an explosion of the powder magazine in nearby Castel Sant' Angelo shattered two small sections of the ceiling.

Although no serious structural damage occurred over the years, humidity, water leakage from the roof, candle soot, dust, and glue from various restoration efforts hastened the deterioration of the artwork, in some cases significantly. Descriptions from visitors who viewed the artwork in the years immediately following its completion and many years later confirm the steady decline.

In 1588, only forty-seven years after the artwork was completed, author Pompeo Ugonio described the vivid colors and intricate scenes that greeted chapel visitors in the first-known published description of the chapel:

> All the rest [of the walls and vaults] is distinguished by various images executed in lively colors, and by the hand of excellent painters. Among them are the effigies of those Kings and Patriarchs from whom the Virgin Mary and our Savior descended, together with the mysteries pertaining to the nativity of Christ; and raising one's eyes to the canopy which is in the form of a circular vault, we see the Angelic hierarchies which bow reverently to the very holy Presepio that is concealed here inside [the chapel].[33]

By 1768, however, the luster was gone, and the colors were hard to distinguish, as demonstrated by this description from a French traveler who visited the chapel: "The whole ceiling . . . is monotonous, its colour tends towards dull red and grey; however, this defect is compensated by the design."[34]

Goethe, who much admired the artwork of the chapel when he visited it in 1786, also commented on its condition and accurately foretold its future:

> On 2nd February we went to the Sistine Chapel to witness the ceremony of the blessing of the candles. . . . I thought . . . it is precisely these candles that over three centuries have blackened these splendid frescoes; this is the incense that . . . has not only with its smoke covered over the sun itself of art, but with every year continues to dirty it and will finally engulf it in darkness.[35]

Keeping the chapel clean had always been a problem. According to church records, in 1543 Pope Paul III created the office of mundator, or cleaner, charged with the responsibility of

> cleaning away the dust and other kinds of dirt, as previously mentioned, from the paintings in the said chapel of Sixtus, both those on the ceiling of events fulfilled and those on the wall of events prophesied, and to make all efforts to keep them free from dirt.[36]

Visitors tour the Sistine Chapel in the mid–nineteenth century. Over the centuries, the paintings accumulated layers of dirt, dust, and candle soot.

In 1543, Pope Paul III created the office of mundator to keep the paintings clean.

EARLY RESTORATION EFFORTS

Various attempts had been made over the centuries to clean and restore the artwork, but the results were poor. A complete cleaning of the chapel took place in 1625, although this effort consisted of little more than dusting the ceiling with a linen cloth and pressing it with moistened bread to remove any remaining dirt.

In the ensuing years, other restoration projects were also undertaken. However well intentioned, these projects actually did more harm than good. The first recorded restoration effort, and the most damaging, took place between 1710 and 1712. Moistened bread was rubbed carefully over the surface to clean it, then a layer of varnish or glue made from animal fats was spread (sometimes in a haphazard fashion) over the frescoes in an attempt to freshen and deepen the fading colors and to serve as a protective layer. Humidity eventually caused these layers to break down, shrink, curl, crack, and even pull some of the fresco away from the ceiling itself. Other restoration and cleaning was done during 1762, 1895, 1904–1905, and 1936–1938.

AN AMBITIOUS UNDERTAKING

By the 1960s, art experts—both independent and connected to the Vatican—determined that a careful cleaning and restoration using the most modern techniques available was necessary to prevent the masterpieces from being lost forever. There was great concern over attempting this on such treasured artwork. The goal was to reverse the effects of centuries of gradual damage. It would be the most ambitious art restoration project in history.

The project initially involved only the frescoes on the side walls, those depicting the lives of Moses and Christ. The side walls (including the lunettes) were so dirty that it was generally assumed that no thorough cleaning had been attempted for centuries, possibly since their execution. The side frescoes were cleaned with great success between 1964 and 1974, revealing the inscriptions in the frieze above them, which had been covered over by dirt and forgotten. The restoration was so successful that the team continued its work moving on to different sections of the chapel.

In 1975 cleaning of the faux draperies revealed that they had been entirely painted over using the *a secco* method, and they were subsequently restored to their original design. The two entrance frescoes painted by Matteo da Lecce and Hendrick van der Broeck were also cleaned and restored. This proved a difficult proposition as much of the work was also painted *a secco* and was inferior to the rest of the chapel's frescoes. Some portions had also been altered in later years, and earlier cleaning efforts had damaged the panels. Although great care was taken during the modern restoration, the results were poor, leaving the frescoes blurred and grayed. The restoration experts decided to leave the altered portions as they were to avoid further deterioration.

In 1980 the restoration team carried out a series of tests to determine if Michelangelo's frescoes should also be cleaned and restored. These tests revealed the cracking and curling of the surface due to the animal glue and also the damage from rainwater. Small portions of one of his lunettes were successfully cleaned, revealing the beautiful colors of Michelangelo's pigments. His work had been obscured to such a degree that art scholars for decades had incorrectly believed that Michelangelo, although gifted in design, had no artistic sense of color. These revelations convinced experts that a full restoration of the chapel's artwork was possible and desirable.

The Vatican and its restoration team publicly announced their intentions in 1981. The precious ceiling frescoes and *The Last Judgment* would be cleaned and fully restored. It was estimated that the project would take more than a decade to complete.

Objections were immediately voiced by a small group of artists and critics who did not want the ceiling touched in any manner. They felt that Michelangelo's work should remain as it was, fearing that any restoration efforts would destroy it. Letters were sent to the Vatican begging officials to discontinue the project. One artist of international renown, Andy Warhol, who was known as a leader of the pop art movement, lent his support to this group shortly before he died. Although the work continued unhindered, the Vatican did not want to be in the center of controversy.

The Vatican, the restoration team, and the multitude of scholars and others involved took great care to allay the fears of their critics. They determined that the entire process was to be

A LETTER OF PROTEST

In a letter to Pope John Paul II, fourteen American artists protested the restoration effort. An excerpt of that letter appears in Waldemar Januszczak's book *Sayonara, Michelangelo: The Sistine Chapel Restored and Repackaged.*

We fully recognize the noble purpose of those who have authorized the restoration . . . and the extensive research that was undertaken in preparation for the task. We respectfully propose a pause in the restoration, however, to allow a thorough analysis of the results obtained so far. This precautionary measure would provide an opportunity to review all of the options available for the continued preservation of this master work.

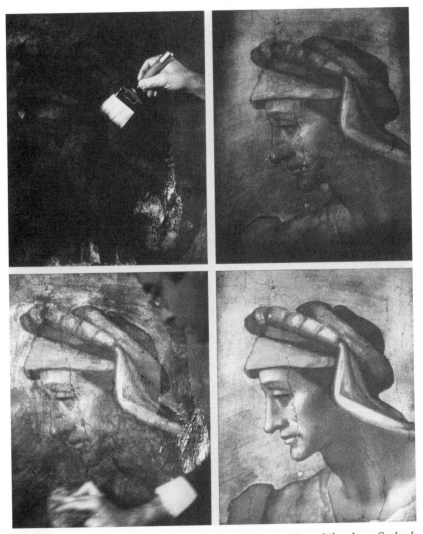

Four photos show the progression of cleaning a portion of the Azor-Sadoch lunette.

documented, and its progress would be shared with the art world. Over fifteen thousand photographs were taken throughout the restoration, and the process was filmed by the Nippon Television Network Corporation of Japan. An international examining committee, requested by the Vatican, monitored all stages of the work.

Knowing the importance of the priceless works being restored, great care had been taken to preserve Michelangelo's work in its original condition. As an example, in the lunette of Naason, the woman gazing into a mirror, a new base for the panel had been painted in the eighteenth century because the area had been covered by scaffolding when Michelangelo was painting it. The base was removed and left with the unfinished rough outline that Michelangelo had painted himself. Preparations to begin work on the ceiling went forward.

THE SCAFFOLDING IS ERECTED

A special lightweight aluminum scaffolding was built according to Michelangelo's own design (which was so successfully employed in 1508), and its supports were placed in the exact same holes in the walls that were originally used. Because the scaffolding covered an area only approximately six yards wide, the chapel remained open during the entire restoration, and the progress could be viewed by visitors from below. Although the scaffolding was closed for security reasons to the general public, art experts and restorers were granted regular access to it,

A restoration expert works atop scaffolding erected for restoration of ceiling frescoes. The modern scaffolding was a replica of Michelangelo's original design.

which gave them a once-in-a-lifetime, up-close view of the masterpiece. It also served to reassure skeptics of the success of the project as it progressed.

Restoration experts had to determine exactly what type of pigments they were dealing with to avoid damaging them during cleaning. They also had to determine the stability of the plaster. Innumerable tests were carried out on the surface of the ceiling before any work was done. The surface was studied in many different ways; a syringe was used to check the content and depth of the plaster, and observations were also taken with highly sophisticated microscopes in various types of lighting. Samples of the pigments (small flakes of paint) were taken for laboratory analysis to determine their chemical makeup.

CLEANING METHODS

The cleaning of the ceiling began in late 1984. Although success on the wall frescoes gave the restorers confidence, the pressure of working on Michelangelo's famous frescoes was enormous. The methods used were precise and complicated. A solvent mixture known as AB57, which had been in use for some time for cleaning artwork, was adopted for the ceiling. The mixture acts instantly. Applied by hand in a painstakingly careful fashion, it was allowed to remain on the area to be cleaned for only about three minutes. It was then removed with a natural sponge that had been sterilized and soaked in twice-distilled water. In extremely dirty areas, the process would be repeated in twenty-four hours when deemed necessary.

The few *a secco* portions were treated differently because they were more delicate and sensitive to water. In these cases, the frescoes were cleaned with organic solvents.

The ceiling frescoes were found to be in a generally good state of conservation. Any minor touch-ups needed were done in watercolors and were carefully blended with crosshatched brush strokes. These were done only when absolutely necessary. After removing many layers of dirt and glue, the final layer of dust— which had probably settled on the fresco during the first year of its life—was left untouched, keeping the fresco exactly as Michelangelo left it. No preservatives of any kind were applied.

The restoration's many revelations put some critics' claims to rest. Art conservator Gianluigi Colalucci wrote to the *Washington Post* regarding critics who insisted that Michelangelo himself

A PARTY ON THE PLATFORM

Gianluigi Colalucci, the chief restorer of the Sistine Chapel project, became very familiar with Michelangelo's work. Colalucci actually spent more time on the scaffolding during the painstaking restoration than Michelangelo himself when he executed the paintings. Colalucci also took part in a special celebration on the platform. In Bart McDowell's book *Inside the Vatican,* Colalucci shares some of his thoughts about the multitalented artist and the celebration that took place inches below the renowned masterpiece: "His brush strokes are like his signature—done like a sculptor. And his sculpture is like architecture. All his skills are one."

During a party on the scaffolding in December 1989, Colalucci undertook a very special bit of cleaning: the space between the nearly touching fingers of Adam and God, the most well-known portion of the entire ceiling. In a dramatic and unforgettable moment, as the few guests present applauded, he carefully cleaned the barrier between the human and divine "and we hoped the scaffold would not fall."

applied varnish to his own work and that restorers were removing the artist's intended protective layer:

> How could a man of genius, a man who was a master of his technique, ever have sought to dim and darken such lifelike beauty? . . . [The critics] are playing on a public that likes things mysterious. They don't seem to know painting a fresco is a simple but very precise technique. We know how it was done, and we are doing nothing at all to harm it.[37]

The cleaning and restoration of the ceiling was completed on December 31, 1989, one year longer than originally projected. The project is estimated to have required thirty thousand hours of work.

THE LAST JUDGMENT

The process of restoring and cleaning *The Last Judgment* began early in 1990. A huge scaffolding with seven work platforms was built to allow access to every bit of surface area of the massive fresco. Unfortunately, the fresco would remain hidden by the scaffolding during the entire restoration.

The Last Judgment, which lacked the painted architectural divisions of the ceiling, could not be separated into sections for cleaning. Therefore, thorough preliminary tests, taking more than a year to complete, were conducted on every level of the fresco to study its surface before cleaning began. The tests revealed many differences in technique compared with those used on the ceiling. The large amount of lapis lazuli, the delicate color used for the blue of the sky; the use of some paints such as vegetable lacquer and *giallolino,* which required the use of a binding agent; and *a secco* portions of the fresco posed difficult problems in cleaning and called for a different method than the one used for the ceiling.

The fresco also showed a great deal of retouching and repainting, possibly because it was in a much more accessible location than the ceiling. It was decided that the "breeches" added to cover some of the nudes would be removed when they were deemed not original to Michelangelo's work.

THE CLEANING METHOD OF *THE LAST JUDGMENT*

The preliminary washing was done with distilled water only. The area being cleaned was then treated with a solution of water and 25 percent ammonium carbonate, alternated with nitrate thinner. After twenty-four hours, the ammonium carbonate was reapplied through four layers of Japanese paper and was left on for about nine minutes. The paper was then removed and the area was cleaned with a sponge soaked in the same solution. Further washings with distilled water were carried out when necessary. Great care was taken to ensure that the fresco was cleaned without rubbing or friction, especially on the lapis lazuli of the

Gianluigi Colalucci restores a section of The Last Judgment *near the charon's boat.*

sky. The ammonium carbonate was also left on for a shorter period of time on those delicate areas.

DAMAGE AND IMPERFECTIONS ARE REVEALED

The cleaning revealed damage to the painting, which was known through historical sources but was not previously visible. In the early 1800s Vincenzo Camuccini noted damage to the sky above the group of souls rising from the dead and the charon's barge. He reported "There was once a time when unintentionally they tried to destroy this masterpiece by applying a strong corrosive agent across the entire painting."[38] The application of the corrosive agent was confirmed during the restoration, but the date of application remains unclear.

The modern restoration revealed uneven coloration of the fresco but also an intensity, depth, and beauty to the pigments not seen for generations. Scholars have debated why areas of color are uneven and have suggested various possibilities. For example, some colors stand the test of time better than others. Other possible causes include damages from fungus, foreign matter such as dirt, or glue and vegetable oils applied during previous restorations.

The restoration also revealed the *giornates* indicating how large an area Michelangelo painted at certain times and how quickly he worked on those areas. This finding was of particular interest to art scholars studying Michelangelo's work output and placing it in the time frame of when he painted particular portions of the fresco. It also gives a clear picture of the enormous amount of work that the very experienced artist could accomplish during a single day. *Giornate* seams are much more evident on *The Last Judgment* than they are on the ceiling, possibly because past restorations and the abrasion of frequent dustings have worn away any finishing touches meant to disguise them. *The Last Judgment* included more than 450 *giornates*.

Although the fresco is well preserved, alterations over the centuries have left various portions of its surface in different states of conservation. As with the ceiling, no preservatives were applied to the fresco. The restoration of *The Last Judgment* was completed in 1994.

A GREATER UNDERSTANDING OF THE ARTIST'S WORK

In 1986 with the help of digital computer images, experts were able to chart the restoration, the state of preservation of the

The restoration of The Last Judgment *revealed many* giornates. *Here, Gianluigi Colalucci works on a portion of the enormous fresco just to the right of Christ.*

frescoes, and some of the techniques employed by Michelangelo on the ceiling and *The Last Judgment.* The computer technology made it possible to chart the artist's progress for the first time, giving the modern world a true picture of the massive amount of work he accomplished. His brush strokes were also analyzed, showing a man whose confidence evolved as the project progressed, allowing him to paint more and more swiftly.

The restoration also revealed the areas on which the cartoons had been pounced and on which they had been incised. The random pattern of pouncing and depth of incising also served as proof that many different assistants had helped with the menial labor.

Computer analysis of the pigments also revealed not only their variety but also their content. This information had been unknown in modern times and had only been briefly described in the writings of past artists and craftsmen. The restoration also allowed the corrections and *a secco* work to be viewed clearly for the first time. Preserved and restored to their original glory, the frescoes revealed Michelangelo's true genius as a colorist to the modern world.

A group of respected art conservators invited by the Vatican to study the restorations reported, "The new freshness of the colors and the clarity of the forms on the Sistine ceiling are totally in keeping with 16th century painting and affirm the full majesty and splendour of Michelangelo's creation."[39]

The group also agreed with the Vatican that the true colors of the frescoes had been "obscured by uneven layers of soot, glue, salt deposits and numerous previous restorations," and that "all these conditions combine to falsify the grandeur of Michelangelo's intention by flattening the forms and reducing the colors to a monochrome that has mislead generations."[40]

THE FINAL CHALLENGE

The successful restoration of the invaluable frescoes, a project that took thirty years to accomplish, marked only the beginning of what the Vatican hoped to achieve. The final challenge remained to control the environment of the frescoes to maintain their state of preservation. This challenge was researched during the mid-1980s to determine possible solutions. The biggest problems were the dust and dirt that was brought in by the millions of tourists who visited the chapel each year (one day alone

A computer image of the ceiling fresco The Temptation and Fall of Adam. *Computers allowed restorers to view Michelangelo's techniques.*

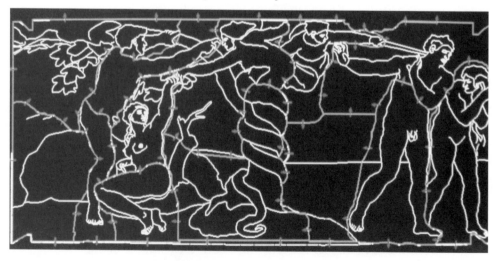

TECHNOLOGY AS THE ANSWER TO EVERYTHING

Author and artist Robin Richmond explains her views on the restoration project in the introduction of her book *Michelangelo and the Creation of the Sistine Chapel.* Her feelings were shared by many, as was her change of heart as the restoration progressed.

When I heard about the restoration of the Sistine Chapel, I thought: "Here they go again, using technology as the answer to everything. The whiter than white school of art history. Painting as laundry." Like many artists, I felt that a great master's art must remain forever untouched by the "evils" of science. It is a common prejudice of artists. There were many who considered that the restoration obliterated Michelangelo's final intentions and would remove his touch.

After many visits to the scaffolding in the Sistine Chapel, spent looking at and even touching the ceiling, I am convinced that this view was wrong. I have examined the facts and discussed the restoration extensively with the Vatican technicians and scientists over many years, and am persuaded that what I and other much greater scholars thought of as Michelangelo's gloomy, dark and melancholy painting style is the accumulation of almost five hundred years of soot, grime and misguided human interference.

during the summer of 1989 nineteen thousand visitors were recorded) and the humidity, noxious gases, and other pollutants in the air.

To combat the first problem, a special carpet was installed to retain the dust and dirt brought in by visitors. New lighting was also installed and was positioned to elude rising air currents and to properly illuminate the frescoes without harming them.

A special air filtering and conditioning system was put in place to control the temperature and eliminate the humidity problem. This complex system was designed and installed by the Carrier Corporation of Connecticut. The system uses an

Protective measures preserve the Sistine Chapel and allow millions of tourists each year to enjoy the building and its masterpieces.

optical-chilled mirror to measure the humidity and keep it at a precise 55 percent. Condensation that forms on the mirror's surface is measured with the use of a sophisticated device called a photodetector. A platinum resistance thermometer, which is embedded just below the mirror's surface, measures the mirror's temperature. Any changes in the dew point are automatically detected, and the humidity is immediately adjusted.

The small, unobtrusive sensors are located high on the chapel wall and in the ceiling itself. The system is easy to maintain and will relay a signal if the sensors require service. The challenge of creating and keeping a proper environment for the frescoes was met and successfully resolved with the use of the latest modern technology.

The Restoration Is Revealed

A special mass was celebrated on the morning of April 8, 1994, at the reopening of the newly restored chapel. After the procession arrived at the foot of the altar, the lights were turned on, revealing the artwork. Members of the congregation were silent, awed by the magnificence of the scene before them.

The great work of the master artists had been rediscovered and reintroduced to the modern age. The most ambitious art restoration of the century returned an immeasurable glory to the inspiring and most holy chapel. The Sistine Chapel and its famous frescoes have been preserved for generations to come.

NOTES

Chapter 1: The Pope's Chapel

1. Pierluigi de Vecchi, ed., *The Sistine Chapel: A Glorious Restoration*. New York: Harry N. Abrams, 1992, p. 259.
2. Quoted in de Vecchi, *The Sistine Chapel*, p. 258.
3. Quoted in Steven F. Ostrow, *Art and Spirituality in Counter-Reformation Rome*. New York: Cambridge University Press, 1996, p. 3.

Chapter 2: The Wall Frescoes

4. Quoted in Francesco Papafava, ed., *The Sistine Chapel*. Florence, Italy: Monumenti, Musei E Gallerie Pontificie, SCALA, 1986, p. 10.
5. Quoted in Evelyn March Phillips, *The Frescoes in the Sistine Chapel*, London: John Murray, 1907. p. 13.
6. Quoted in John T. Paoletti and Gary M. Radke, *Art in Renaissance Italy*. New York: Harry N. Abrams, 1997, p. 306.

Chapter 3: Michelangelo and the Sistine Chapel Ceiling

7. Quoted in Rick Bromer, "Pope Picks Michelangelo to Paint Ceiling." http://ourworld.compuserve.com/homepages/OLDNEWS/sistine.htm.
8. Quoted in D. Redig de Campos, *The Sistine Chapel*. New York: Reynal, n.d., p. 2.
9. Quoted in de Vecchi, *The Sistine Chapel*, p. 46.
10. Quoted in Robin Richmond, *Michelangelo and the Creation of the Sistine Chapel Ceiling*. New York: Crescent Books, 1993, p. 147.
11. Quoted in George Bull, *Michelangelo*. New York: St. Martin's, 1995, p. 95.
12. Quoted in de Vecchi, *The Sistine Chapel*, p. 180.
13. Quoted in Charles Seymour Jr., ed., *Michelangelo and the Sistine Chapel Ceiling*. New York: W. W. Norton, 1972, p. 93.
14. Quoted in Carlo Pietrangelli, *The Sistine Chapel: The Art, the History, and the Restoration*. New York: Harmony Books, 1986, p. 256.
15. Quoted in Bull, *Michelangelo*, p.104.
16. Quoted in Richmond, *Michelangelo and the Creation of the Sistine Chapel Ceiling*, p. 147.
17. Quoted in Robert J. Clements, ed., *Michelangelo, a Self-Portrait*. Englewood Cliffs, NJ: Prentice-Hall, 1963, p. 144.

18. Quoted in de Vecchi, *The Sistine Chapel*, p. 39.

19. Quoted in Bromer, "Pope Picks Michelangelo to Paint Ceiling."

20. Quoted in Oreste Ferrari, *Masterpieces of the Vatican*. New York: Harry N. Abrams, 1971, p.174.

Chapter 4: The Last Judgment

21. Quoted in Fabrizio Mancinelli, *The Sistine Chapel*, trans. Henry McConnachie. Vatican City: Edizioni Musei Vaticani, 1993, p. 80.

22. Quoted in Mancinelli, *The Sistine Chapel*, p. 80.

23. Quoted in Pietrangelli, *The Sistine Chapel*, p. 78.

24. Phillips, *The Frescoes in the Sistine Chapel*, p. 141.

25. Quoted in Papafava, *The Sistine Chapel*, p. 89.

26. Quoted in A. Lipinsky, *The Vatican*. New York: Doubleday, 1968, p. 78.

27. Quoted in Lipinsky, *The Vatican*, p. 79.

28. Quoted in Pietrangelli, *The Sistine Chapel*, p. 190.

29. Quoted in Mancinelli, *The Sistine Chapel*, p. 89.

30. Phillips, *The Frescoes in the Sistine Chapel*, p. 131.

31. Quoted in de Vecchi, *The Sistine Chapel*, p. 238.

32. Quoted in Manfred Wundram, *Paintings of the Renaissance*. New York: Taschen, 1997, p. 98.

Chapter 5: Historic Restorations

33. Quoted in Ostrow, *Art and Spirituality in Counter-Reformation Rome*, p. 63.

34. Quoted in Pietrangelli, *The Sistine Chapel*, p. 218.

35. Quoted in Pietrangelli, *The Sistine Chapel*, p. 6.

36. Quoted in de Vecchi, *The Sistine Chapel*, p. 236.

37. Quoted in Waldemar Januszczak, *Sayonara, Michelangelo: The Sistine Chapel Restored and Repackaged*. Reading, MA: Addison-Wesley, 1990, p. 187.

38. Quoted in de Vecchi, *The Sistine Chapel*, p. 239.

39. Quoted in Januszczak, *Sayonara, Michelangelo*, p. 184.

40. Quoted in Januszczak, *Sayonara, Michelangelo*, p. 184.

GLOSSARY

arriccio: The preparatory layer of plaster in a fresco that is used to even out the surface to be painted.

a secco: Pigments that must be applied to dry plaster.

balustrade: A row of balusters (upright supports, as in a staircase) topped by a rail.

barrel vault: A roof with a continuous semicircular section.

basilica: A public hall or meeting place. The simple design of basilicas, which features wide central naves, was often used in later chapels and cathedrals.

cartoons: Preparatory drawings done to size and used as guides in painting; sometimes transferred directly to the area to be painted.

choir: The part of a church or cathedral that is occupied by singers.

corbel: The bracket that projects from a wall to support weight.

cornice: The horizontal, projecting portion that crowns the wall of a building.

crenellation: A battlement; a decorative or defensive parapet on top of a wall.

foreshortening: To shorten details in a drawing so it appears to have depth.

fresco: The technique of painting directly onto wet plaster; the painting itself is also called a fresco.

frieze: An ornamental band, often sculptured, extending around a room or building.

garzoni: Assistants.

giornate: The section of a fresco that can be painted in one day's work.

indirect incision: The method by which a drawing or cartoon is laid directly onto wet plaster and the contours are traced with a metal or ivory stylus, producing an outline. Tracing too deeply ruins the surface of the plaster, but this method is quicker to execute than pouncing.

intonaco: The upper layer of plaster in a fresco to which paint is applied.

lintel: A horizontal piece across the top of an opening (such as a door) that carries the weight of the structure above it.

lunette: One of the rounded compositions immediately over the windows.

medallion: A circular disk painted with design in imitation of bronze gilt.

pigment: Any coloring matter; during the Renaissance painting pigments were derived from mineral and vegetable sources.

pouncing: The method by which a detailed drawing is placed over a second sheet that is meant to be destroyed and imbedded in wet plaster. The top sheet is then used as a guide for the stylus. Small holes are punctured into the paper and hit with a small bag of charcoal dust, leaving the outline of the design in the plaster. This method leaves the surface to be painted flat and undamaged.

pozzolana: A finely ground volcanic powder used in *intonaco* in the fresco process.

vault: An arched covering, usually in masonry, over any part of a building.

For Further Reading

David J. Brown, *How Things Were Built*. New York: Random House, 1992. Detailed illustrations enhance this book, which covers more than sixty famous structures—from ancient to modern times—explaining construction methods and providing an excellent glossary of architectural terms.

Nathaniel Harris, *Renaissance Art*. New York: Thomson Learning, 1994. A complete and easy-to-read overview explaining the Renaissance movement and the art and architecture of the times.

David Jacobs, *Master Builders of the Middle Ages*. New York: Harper and Row, 1969. An interesting look at the building methods up to the 1400s. Although predating work on the Sistine Chapel, this book explains the role of many craftsmen—carpenters, stained glass makers, tapestry weavers, masons, and others—who contribute greatly but whose work is often anonymous.

Michelangelo: The Sistine Chapel. New York: Wings Books, 1992. A simple guide with color plates of many sections of the famous ceiling and a short biography of the artist.

Ernest Raboff, *Michelangelo Buonarroti*. New York: Doubleday, n.d. An easy-to-read, illustrated biography and overview of all of Michelangelo's most famous works.

Works Consulted

Robert Adams, *The Lost Museum*. New York: Viking, 1980. A lavishly illustrated, detailed book documenting thousands of vanished art treasures, from ancient civilizations, the Renaissance, and today, known only by copies made from the masters' original works or descriptions.

Guilo Carlo Argan and Bruno Contardi, *Michelangelo, Architect*. New York: Harry N. Abrams, 1993. A detailed volume examining Michelangelo's many architectural designs as well as the faux architectural designs of the Sistine Chapel.

George Bull, *Michelangelo*. New York: St. Martin's, 1995. A comprehensive biography filled with details about the life of Michelangelo as well as insights into the Renaissance.

Robert J. Clements, ed., *Michelangelo, a Self-Portrait*. Englewood Cliffs, NJ: Prentice-Hall, 1963. An engrossing book comprising Michelangelo's own writings and letters.

L. D. Ettlinger, *The Sistine Chapel Before Michelangelo: Religious Imagery and Papal Primacy*. Oxford, Great Britain: Clarendon, 1965. A comprehensive study of frescoes present in the chapel prior to Michelangelo, Pope Sixtus's religious theology, and how the decoration scheme brings both together.

Oreste Ferrari, *Masterpieces of the Vatican*. New York: Harry N. Abrams, 1971. An illustrated volume introducing the Vatican's most famous artworks, including frescoes of the Sistine Chapel.

William Fleming, *Art, Music, and Ideas*. New York: Holt, Rinehart and Winston, 1970. A complete overview of art through the ages—from the ancient world to contemporary styles—with a section featuring Renaissance art, Michelangelo, and his contemporaries.

Waldemar Januszczak, *Sayonara, Michelangelo: The Sistine Chapel Restored and Repackaged*. Reading, MA: Addison-Wesley, 1990. A personal account and critical essay by an art expert who visited the chapel on numerous occasions during the restoration.

A. Lipinsky, *The Vatican*. New York: Doubleday, 1968. A comprehensive guide to the many buildings and art treasures of the Vatican, with color plates of the more famous examples.

Bates Lowry, *Renaissance Architecture*. New York: George Braziller, 1967. A history of architecture, its development as a vehicle of expression for man's philosophy, and papal influences.

Fabrizio Mancinelli, *The Sistine Chapel*. Trans. Henry McConnachie. Vatican City: Edizioni Musei Vaticani, 1993. A comprehensive overview of the chapel, its artwork, and various restoration projects that is complemented by beautiful color prints.

Bart McDowell, *Inside the Vatican*. Washington DC: National Geographic Society, 1991. A fascinating look at famous Vatican City buildings and how the Vatican operates on a daily basis and in world politics.

Steven F. Ostrow, *Art and Spirituality in Counter-Reformation Rome*. New York: Cambridge University Press, 1996. A complex study of the spiritual, political, and social context of chapel art in Rome and its contribution to the papacy as it countered the rising Protestant challenge.

John T. Paoletti and Gary M. Radke, *Art in Renaissance Italy*. New York: Harry N. Abrams, 1997. An immense volume covering Italian art from 1300 to 1530; it also includes political history that influenced the artists as well as thumbnail biographies of dozens of artists and a detailed time line of the period.

Francesco Papafava, ed., *The Sistine Chapel*. Florence, Italy: Monumenti, Musei E Gallerie Pontificie, SCALA, 1986. An illustrated review of the side frescoes, the ceiling, and *The Last Judgment*, with a short chapter on the restoration that was in progress at the time of this printing.

Loren Partridge, *The Sistine Chapel Ceiling, Rome*. New York: George Braziller, 1996. An excellent, fact-filled book covering the history of the chapel, the life of Pope Julius II, and an informative section on fresco techniques.

Evelyn March Phillips, *The Frescoes in the Sistine Chapel*. London: John Murray, 1907. A comprehensive overview of the side frescoes, ceiling frescoes, and tapestries of the Sistine Chapel.

Carlo Pietrangelli, *The Sistine Chapel: The Art, the History, and the Restoration*. New York: Harmony Books, 1986. A beautifully illustrated and detailed book covering the papal history of the chapel and its artwork as well as an in-depth look at the frescoes and their restoration.

D. Redig de Campos, *The Sistine Chapel*. New York: Reynal, n.d. An art book with large color plates and detailed descriptions, including stories about the origins and inspiration for works of art, whether biblical or otherwise.

Robin Richmond, *Michelangelo and the Creation of the Sistine Chapel Ceiling*. New York: Crescent Books, 1993. An excellent, highly readable book delving into Michelangelo's personal history as well as the dramatic elements of the painting of the ceiling—from techniques to religious interpretation and the twentieth-century restoration process.

Roberto Salvini et al., *Vatican Museums Rome*. New York: Newsweek and Arnoldo Mondadori Editore, 1968. A complete study of the buildings and art treasures of Vatican City.

Paul Schubring, *The Sistine Chapel*. Rome, Italy: J. Frank & O. Dittmann, 1910. Detailed essays and critiques covering architectural aspects of the chapel as well as the famous artwork; illustrated with numerous black-and-white prints.

Charles Seymour Jr., ed., *Michelangelo and the Sistine Chapel Ceiling*. New York: W. W. Norton, 1972. An excellent book offering a chronological history of the ceiling as well as excerpts from original documents, a study of biblical references, and critical essays.

Charles de Tolnay, *Michelangelo*. Trans. Gaynor Woodhouse. Princeton, NJ: Princeton University Press, 1975. Originally published in the 1940s, this five-volume series remains the most comprehensive and authoritative work on Michelangelo. More attention is given to discussion of the artist's works than details of his life. Contains photographs of every work by Michelangelo.

Charles de Tolnay, *The Sistine Chapel*. Princeton, NJ: Princeton University Press, 1949. A book of general information focusing on the architectural design of the chapel being integrated into Michelangelo's plan for the fresco placements.

Pierluigi de Vecchi, ed., *The Sistine Chapel: A Glorious Restoration.* New York: Harry N. Abrams, 1992. An in-depth account of the restoration of the Sistine Chapel, which took place during the 1980s, featuring large, beatifully photographed color plates of the famous artworks.

Manfred Wundram, *Paintings of the Renaissance.* New York: Taschen, 1997. Beautiful color photographs enhance this detailed book of Renaissance artworks, which are grouped by their country of origin; biographies of the artists are included.

Internet Source

Rick Bromer, "Pope Picks Michelangelo to Paint Ceiling." http://ourworld.compuserve.com/homepages/OLDNEWS/sistine.htm. This site contains chapel history as well as this excellent article pertaining to the painting of the ceiling.

INDEX

PICTURE CREDITS

Cover photos: (large) Art Resource, (small) Planet Art, (gear) Vittoriano Rastelli/Corbis

Archive Photos, 25, 35, 47

AKG London, 26, 68

Alinari/Art Resource, 18

Art Resource, 22, 42

Corbis, 21, 79

Corbis/Bettmann, 10, 48, 67

Corbis/Bettmann/UPI, 71

David Lees/Corbis, 60

Vittoriano Rastelli/Corbis, 72, 75, 77, 78

North Wind, 46, 54

Planet Art, 30, 38, 45, 65

Prints Old And Rare, 16

Scala/Art Resource, 29, 31, 32, 51, 59, 61

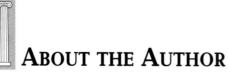

ABOUT THE AUTHOR

Renee C. Rebman is a published playwright, actress, and director at her local community theater. She is also active with local schools, serving as a coordinator and presenter for the Picture Person Program, a volunteer art-enrichment program. She lives in Lexington, Ohio, with her daughter, Scarlett, and her son, Roddy. *The Sistine Chapel* is her third nonfiction book.